WIN THE DAY

COURAGE, POSITIVE THINKING AND THE WARRIOR SPIRIT

WIN THE DAY

COURAGE, POSITIVE THINKING AND THE WARRIOR SPIRIT

José Semedo and Sam Kotadia

Win The Day®

First published in June 2015 by Mindsport Ltd

Win The Day is a registered trademark in the United Kingdom

Cover image and copyright of the cover provided by Steve Ellis

Editorial provided by Caroline Sheldrick

Designed and typeset by Mach 3 Solutions Ltd, Stroud, Gloucestershire

Printed and bound by Imago Publishing Ltd, Oxford, UK

To Cristiano Ronaldo
It if wasn't for your kindness I may never have made it as a professional footballer. I'm eternally grateful, thank you so much.
José Semedo

To Lucy Hill
With love and more importantly thanks for putting up with the endless psychological spiel over the last year!
Sam Kotadia

CONTENTS

FOREWORD

I had the pleasure of starting my career in football with Semedo. From our early years we have been like brothers, and always supported one another to work hard and give our best. Although we now play for different teams, in heart and mind we are on this footballing journey together.

Win The Day shows just how dedicated José is to being the best he can be, both as a professional and as a person. The book also reminds me of José's big heart and his desire to help and support other people so they can reach their full potential.

I'm sure Semedo will inspire younger players with his wise words and stories about his priceless experiences in the world of football. I wish him every success with the launch of his book.

Cheers, bro!
Cristiano Ronaldo

BIOGRAPHIES

José Semedo

Born in Portugal, José Semedo started his footballing career at Sporting Lisbon, another product of their prolific youth system. Soon after establishing himself in their youth academy, José made his professional debut for Lisbon-based football club Casa Pia AC. This led on to several loan moves abroad where he played for clubs including CD Feirense and the Italian Serie A club Cagliari.

In 2007 José signed for Charlton Athletic on a four-year deal. Although the club initially saw him as a central defender, he soon found his feet as a defensive midfielder. Towards the end of his contract for Charlton in 2011, José was crowned Charlton's Player of the Year after receiving 43% of the votes. Despite winning this there were no assurances José would have his contract renewed and this led to his move to Sheffield Wednesday, then managed by Gary Megson. In his first year under Megson, he was crowned Wednesday's Player of the Year as well as receiving the League One PFA Fans' Player of the Year award.

José has publicly announced that Sheffield Wednesday is his 'home' and that he was destined to play for the club. He continues to play for Sheffield Wednesday after agreeing a new deal in 2015.

His journey through football has been heavily shaped by the influence and support of childhood friend and former team-mate Cristiano Ronaldo. The motivation and inspiration of Ronaldo drove him to explore the inner depths of his own psyche in the hunt for self-improvement. This led to seven years of intensive work with sport psychologist Sam Kotadia where José developed new healthy perspectives on sport and on life in general.

It was in the summer of July 2013 that José and Sam decided to work together in writing *Win the Day*. Sharing José's thought-provoking insights and experiences from the world of sport, the book portrays how developing a winning mental attitude is not just reserved for professional athletes, but can help us all.

Sam Kotadia

Sam Kotadia made a name for himself at the age of 22 when he started providing sport psychology support for professional athletes and managers. Graduating from the University of Essex in Psychology and Sport Science, Sam approached Colchester United FC to offer his services as a sport psychologist. After three years of support work, Sam forged a close relationship with the club's then manager Phil Parkinson, and helped the team build the winning mentality that won them promotion to the Championship Division. Phil Parkinson continued using Sam's services at Charlton Athletic FC, where he was assigned to help José Semedo rediscover his form. After working with Sam for five years, José received two Player of the Year awards, and a runner-up Player of the Year award at Charlton and his current club Sheffield Wednesday. They continue to work together, pushing the boundaries in positive thinking and personal development.

Over the past decade, having developed leading models of behavioural change and performance improvement, Sam has documented his work in more than 50 publications, ranging from Leadership and Management course books to self-improvement journals. Several of these have been translated into foreign languages by publishing houses abroad, establishing Sam as a respected thought-leader in performance psychology.

Sam now dedicates his time to supporting his private clients and creating new and exciting publications that encourage positive thinking in all walks of life.

ACKNOWLEDGEMENTS

The authors wish to thank the following: Hammy Athwal for your kind support and taking the time to read *Win The Day* – we are glad you enjoyed it; Steve Ellis for allowing us to use such an iconic photo for the front cover – there's no better image for such a project; Robin Hague for your enthusiasm and support in the early stages of the project; Trevor Hill for your priceless review of the book and your attention to detail in the final stages of the project which is much appreciated; Kim McSweeney (Mach 3 Solutions Ltd) for helping us get such a classic look for the book; Paras Mehta for your support which has been invaluable – we are truly grateful; Caroline Sheldrick for your excellent editorial support on this unique project which has exceeded expectations; and Sheffield Wednesday FC – we're both delighted that you're able to support us with the promotion of *Win The Day*. Thank you so much.

PREFACE

The kind act that changed my life

Growing up in Setúbal isn't easy, especially when you are aspiring to be a professional footballer. The odds of making your dreams and ambitions a reality are stacked against you. Setúbal is a suburb of Lisbon that doesn't have the affluence of the capital city. Crime was particularly common in my neighbourhood, so I had hard daily challenges to make smart and healthy choices. Testament to the uphill battle I faced is that many of my friends back home made poor choices and have ended up either in jail or dead!

When I got my break to play for Sporting Lisbon I knew that it would be a battle to keep my place in their youth academy. Unfortunately my first year with Sporting Lisbon didn't go so well for me and consequently they wanted other players to live on site and take my place. I knew that if I had to return to live in my old neighbourhood and spend more time there, whilst trying to become a professional footballer, I would fail or come to a bad end.

At this time I shared a room with Ronaldo and we had managed to build up a close friendship. I remember telling Ronaldo the bad news that I would have to live at home and travel in every day. He told me, 'you cannot go back, they are going to put an extra bed in our room and you are going to stay with us. If you go back we could lose you forever.' He was very insistent and knew my dreams of becoming a top footballer were under threat.

Ronaldo spoke to the boss at Sporting Lisbon and put in a special request. Everyone knew he had a special talent even at that age, which meant influential people in the club would listen to him. Fortunately for me, they did. Thinking back, I remember the size of the room we had to sleep in and how difficult it was to put in an extra bed; it was not easy.

From that point onwards everything in my life changed for the better. I will always cherish this act of kindness from my friend. It will stay with me forever.

My heartbeat

My family know how important they are to me in my life. A day doesn't go by when I am not thinking about them. My wife, my children, my mum, my dad, my brothers and sisters – they are always in my heart. Whenever I can I always try to help them and be there for them. Family is everything to me.

I always put my family first because I want to make them happy. Irrespective of how well I'm doing in football, if my family are not happy then I'm not happy.

When I come home to see my boys and my wife the feeling is overwhelming. The love I feel for them seems to get stronger every time I see them. It doesn't matter what has happened out on the football pitch, when I come home to my family everything is put into perspective. It's the best feeling in the world. It is hard, so hard, to describe what I feel for them. My words do not do justice to the love I have for my family.

INTRODUCTION

The mission

During my career as a footballer I've learned a lot which has helped me develop as a player and also as a person. I believe learning is a continual process that should go on throughout our lives.

I was the least talented of the players in our 1985 year group at Sporting Lisbon. Fortunately for me, the influence of my friend Ronaldo during our early years growing up together in Portugal gave me a hunger to be the best I can be at all times. When you are privileged to share some of your first footballing experiences with the greatest footballer on the planet, it fires up your own ambition and hunger to be the best you can be.

One of the areas that I've been motivated to explore and invest time in is the role of psychology in football, and more importantly how I can use it to get better. My commitment over the last six years to examine my inner game and new ways to improve has given me a wholly different perspective on what it means to be successful. It has also encouraged me to reflect on the profound effect of growing up with Ronaldo. I'm hoping my experiences are of value not only to athletes but for all of us, in the different paths we follow in our lives and the various challenges we face.

You don't have to be an expert in psychology or up there with Cristiano in ability to benefit from what I've learned over the years. Everyone can share in these experiences.

Although everything I've learned centres on the football arena, I believe these ideas can be used in all walks of life. Professional football puts you under the spotlight. You cannot escape the ups and downs, constant drama, surprise, excitement and disappointments. Football uses all of the emotions that you experience day to day, condensed down to 90 minutes, sometimes with extra time and a penalty shoot-out!

At the elite level of any sport, the margin for error is tiny. Mental toughness is often the difference between the athletes who win and lose. But learning to master the mind and to control emotions can very easily be ignored because unfortunately it is often not considered an essential part of an athlete's professional lifestyle. It is an aspect of life you believe you don't need to address, because without it you can still function. The mind is like a silent computer running in the background, usually without our awareness.

Part of my psychological journey led me to realise the importance of a 'warrior mentality' in sport and life. Being a warrior for me is about being proactive as opposed to being reactive. It is about challenging yourself every day, and fighting to make each day count. It is about being true to yourself and leading an honest life with integrity. It is about winning the day.

I hope the book captures this and inspires YOU to be positive and make every moment count.

The journey

The first chapter of the book, 'Knowing myself', talks about the main reason I wanted to learn more about sport psychology and how the desire to better myself was sparked by my relationship with Ronaldo. I also talk about Phil Parkinson, who helped me to build my intensity as a player and hunger to leave no stone unturned in my drive to improve.

The second chapter is called 'The inner battle', and is concerned with knowing your enemy. It paints a clear picture of the psychological and mental challenges that I've always faced. It lays out my battlefield and describes what I'm confronted with inside the sporting arena. Being able to share my journey with Ronaldo in professional sport reminds me that all the challenges mentioned in this section are universal, whatever level you are playing at in the professional game.

My own mental enemies include: managing expectations; avoiding becoming pre-occupied with successes and failures; dealing with the day-to-day events that are out of my control; and managing the social pressures in professional football. Even outside of the arena of sport, these are challenges we all face in our own individual lives.

The third chapter shows how important it is for me to get in the right state of mind when preparing for battle. 'The engine room' refers to how I get my core condition and outlook right both before and after performances. It is about being able to control my emotions and keep my mind on the process of being successful as opposed to getting caught up with the positive outcomes that may follow.

The fourth chapter, 'Battle management', explores in depth the areas of mental and personal preparation on which I'm currently focusing. Much of this work concerns pushing myself outside the zone of comfort. It is common to be afraid of making mistakes, but I've learned to take leaps of faith, and challenge myself to take risks regularly. These habits are relevant to people in all walks of life, not just in sport.

The fifth chapter concentrates on mindfulness, which is a popular field these days with various applications in both personal development and healthcare. For me, mindfulness is about developing a clear and honest awareness of the present moment, without getting too lost in my thoughts. My work on mindfulness has had a positive effect on my game as well as improving my day-to-day wellbeing. This chapter includes some detailed explanation of the work I do on developing the warrior mentality and how this applies both to sport and to life.

Forming new habits is hard work, even when you know they are going to be good for you. The sixth chapter, 'Staying on track', looks at some of the tips and tricks I've learned which ensure I stay disciplined and fight to be the best I can be. Forming new habits requires hard work and mental toughness. This is one of the areas of sport psychology support that I found priceless. It is so easy to underestimate how bad habits quickly find their way back into your day-to-day behaviours with very little conscious awareness of them. Fortunately, having Ronaldo as part of my life has helped me to keep my winning mentality sharp.

Having worked hard on my mentality and psychology over the last six years, my attitude towards myself and my general outlook on life have naturally changed. The seventh and final chapter, 'My kind of success', explores my own personal measures of success and what standards I aim to maintain for myself as I continue my professional career. It also honours the mentors and friends who have been so important to me.

In the final section of this introduction, I outline the main lessons that have stuck with me in my journey.

What has stuck

I try to value all of my experiences, in football and in life generally, and do my best to take something positive away from them all. So many experiences have shaped my outlook: leaving home for the first time to carve my way as a professional footballer; fighting my way to secure a professional contract in the game while knowing that I wasn't the most talented; meeting so many kind and inspiring people; managing several injuries along the way and having the unconditional support of an incredible family. These experiences have influenced my overall approach to life.

These are some of the messages that continue to stay with me on my footballing journey. This collection from my early experiences and my later ones form a set of core ideas and approaches that will always be lodged in my mind.

The warrior mentality

At the heart of the warrior mentality, for me, is the ability to pick myself up and get going again: both literally, on the pitch, and in life generally. This approach has kept me 'hungry', wanting more, and has stopped me from hitting the ground during tough times. It's about not giving in and learning to keep going. Bearing this in mind has helped me not to get attached to any one game in particular. Both Ronaldo and I have had a mentality that encourages us to fight for every moment and try to be the best we can be. This is important on and off the football pitch: despite a fall, you don't give up – you pick yourself up and get going again.

Two of the warrior's weapons are will-power and positive thinking. Will-power has been the fuel in my engine room. It has helped me to leave no stone unturned in the fight to be the best I can be in all circumstances.

Whenever I've hit low points, positive thinking has helped me to look at them differently so they serve me as opposed to working against me. I've heard it said that the warrior mentality is like turning straw into gold. For me this sums it up: even what look like wasted opportunities can be precious. All experiences can have purpose and hold value. Knowing this has helped me build deeper foundations for myself and my game. Any footballer can feel confident when things are going their way. The real test of where I am mentally is when things are going against me. How I react is the real measure of whether or not I'm connected with my warrior spirit.

Keeping the flow

Being too attached to the last game – good or bad – is damaging. When my mind is overly focused on a recent good game I put unwanted pressure on myself to make sure I keep the good performances going. On the other hand, when my mind is thinking about a recent poor game I worry that the same performance will follow into the next one. I end up battling with my thoughts and start trying too hard, which breaks my natural flow. Getting stuck or fixated on any one experience has always damaged my game.

This can also happen in training just before games. If I train badly I'm more likely to worry about not being ready for the game, and if I've had an excellent training session I can enter the game over-confident.

'Flow' is about taking experience as it comes, without judgement. This is one of the core ideas in mindfulness. Flow and movement are what give me power on the pitch and in life. With flow, I can ride the highs and lows during a game without getting caught up in any particular experience.

The importance of 'flow' is that it does not discriminate against good and bad, positive or negative, it but it avoids you getting stuck or attached to particular experiences or goals. In life and in sport, I've found power comes when I have movement and momentum. The image which goes with this idea is that of a river.

Flow is lost when I'm pre-occupied with past and future events. My experience of playing every game for Sheffield Wednesday in the 2012/2013 season, in which we won promotion to the Championship, is evidence of what can be achieved by finding flow and maintaining it over a long and hard season. Taking each game as it comes without placing too much importance on it and treating it as another moment is at the heart of achieving flow.

Magical mindfulness

Mindfulness for me is being totally present: soaking up everything that is going on around me and being aware of all physical sensations. When I'm mindfully present in what I'm doing, time stands still and all of my actions become enriched and more precise. Whether it is preparing food or making a tackle on the football pitch, the more absorbed I am in my actions the better they are.

Mindfulness helps me to step out of the immediate dramas that are in front of me and see everything clearly, without judgement. Being aware and conscious of what I'm experiencing has certainly helped me to feel strong in myself and able to deal with most things.

In some ways mindfulness helps me to stop and look at what I have and feel grateful. It helps me to take stock of what is present and not what isn't there. Without mindfulness, life and its amazing experiences can whizz by without me being able to fully appreciate them.

It's a new day

Every day brings new challenges; nothing is ever the same. The moment I think that everything is perfect and going according to plan is the moment I slip back into bad habits. When I'm on a winning streak I'm liable to start taking good performances for granted and consequently lose the attention to detail that resulted in a good performance in the first place. Taking circumstances for granted because of over-confidence has left me stranded when things go wrong.

Central to the work on this journey is 'winning the day'. This is a principle Sam and I came up with to remind me of the dangers of neglecting daily mental practice and not working on the mental routines I've made part of my life. In many ways, the mind requires regular exercise, just like the body, in order to maintain an optimal level of mental fitness. Asking myself whether or not I've won the day keeps me in check and hungry to be the best I can be.

Putting the match day on a pedestal adds unwanted pressure and stops my mind from being truly present in the here-and-now. Reminding myself to 'win the day' is critical in keeping me at my best. It helps me treat every day as a match day. It stops me from getting ahead of myself and helps me squeeze everything out of each moment.

As many of the Sheffield Wednesday fans know, there have been times when I've been left out of the starting line-up for an extended period. When I'm on the side-lines, I find it easy to lose my competitive intensity and edge. With my daily mental training programme and my aim to win the day I've been able to get back into the starting eleven more easily.

Winning the day has kept me mentally sharp, with the right level of motivation to be at my best. Every day is as important as another.

Throughout the book I look at the importance of 'winning the day' and learning to value all of our experiences. The professional journey of sportsmen and women is being able to savour and appreciate not just the big occasions, but also the day-to-day training. This is where athletes spend most of their time, after all, so enjoying these moments is as important as enjoying the big match-day occasions, if not even more.

ONE

KNOWING MYSELF

When I'm true to myself I always play to the best of my ability.

Freedom, passion, honesty, hard work, team-work, loyalty, compassion and a sense of adventure are some of my core personal values. I want to ensure my football life and my performances reflect these personal values. If I can achieve this, I know I can look back on my football career with pride and satisfaction.

From a young age I've always had a certain amount of mental toughness. Growing up in a big family with not a lot of money forced me to appreciate what I have and not take anything for granted. I've learned to be kind, giving and unselfish. Not being spoilt and being brought up by a loving family has no doubt given me a wonderful grounding for living on this planet.

This chapter looks at what sparked my journey to explore my inner game and how understanding my own identity has played its part in shaping my career.

A force of nature

I was only seven when I joined Sporting Lisbon. I was spotted in a local tournament by one of their coaches and picked among five other players from my home town to join their youth academy programme. It was at this time that I truly learned the importance of having a strong identity and sense of self. Moving to a new city, leaving home for the first time and having to make new friends all played a part in toughening me up.

I was fortunate enough to be introduced to Cristiano Ronaldo quite soon after I arrived at Sporting Lisbon. Forming a close friendship with him was critical to me feeling at home and confident enough to play football in the club's prestigious academy. It was in the first training session that we met.

At this time Ronaldo too had to dig deep and find his own identify and mental toughness. When he first arrived in Lisbon, Ronaldo probably had a greater challenge than I did in adjusting to his new life. It was extra hard for Ronaldo because his Madeiran accent was so different that not everyone could understand him. Coming to a new city and being alone for the first time in your life (as I was) – you have to be tough.

Cristiano was also seven years old when he moved to Sporting Lisbon, so it was naturally a big step for him coming as he did from a quiet home town to a busy capital city. In particular both of us were overwhelmed by the size of the shopping centres. There is one large shopping centre in Lisbon called Colombo: it was where everyone wanted to go. At the time it was the biggest in Europe. Compared to what the island of Madeira and Setúbal had to offer, the capital city was another world for us both.

His talent was clear to see from an early age. Everyone wanted to be around him because of his natural gift. Fortunately for me, we developed a deep friendship. At this time, the only thing holding Ronaldo back was that his strength and speed were not yet fully developed. His technical ability was the same as it is today; it is pure natural talent. That's how impressive he was when he arrived at Sporting Lisbon.

Ronaldo played in all of Sporting Lisbon's divisions: Under-15s, 16s, 17s, the B team and the A team. Wherever the important game was, he would be involved. As well as this being an exciting time for him, no doubt he was also tested. In this kind of environment you either sink or swim. And he was a swimmer! Ronaldo's identity and strength of self were, and still are, unmovable. One of my earliest memories is when at the age of ten we entered a tournament together in Portugal. There were always several tournaments at the end of the football season. Before the tournament had even started we knew he was going to be the best player. Predictably he ensured Sporting Lisbon won the tournament and was crowned the best player and the top goal scorer. His mental strength and drive at these points were unbelievable for someone so young. No player went to Sporting Lisbon at our age and impressed the way he did. No one at that age was so courageous on the ball, knew when was the right time to shoot, knew when was the right time to pass and when was the right time to run past players. He had an instinct for the game that no one had ever seen at Sporting Lisbon.

His winning prowess wasn't evident just on the football pitch but in other sports too. We often spent time playing table tennis, table football and snooker and annoyingly he would win them all hands down. It's difficult to understand how someone could be the best at everything he put his mind to. He wouldn't accept losing. Even if you beat him once, he would need to play you again so he would finish on top.

Just being around Ronaldo helped to strengthen my identity on and off the pitch. He has never accepted any negative thinking from me, wanting me always to carry that hunger and positive attitude with me, just as he always does. His self-belief is so high and so strong that when you are in his company he doesn't let your mind go astray. The moment he feels that your mind is starting to feel down he makes your mind rise up again. His approach to football was contagious in a positive way. But no matter how mentally tough you are, few can produce Ronaldo's brilliance on the football pitch.

My first years in football sharpened my resolve to not get ahead of myself and to focus only on working hard: Ronaldo certainly helped with this. With such an appetite for perfection, we both always made sure we gave 100% every day.

If there was a downside, it was that being close to such a great talent, and someone so sure of himself, almost made me feel immune to loss and negative thinking. Combine that with playing for one of the best youth academies in the world and you can understand why feeling positive was easy.

Losing was rare and winning was expected. At times you got the taste of invincibility. Leaving Sporting Lisbon and being put in environments where winning wasn't expected and losing was more common tested my mental toughness. It opened my eyes to the strength of character required to deal with disappointment and regular tension.

The real test

Moving away from Sporting Lisbon was when I had my real test. Suddenly I was no longer enjoying relative comfort but was out in the harsh world of professional football. My best friend had now stepped through the gears and was progressing rapidly in the world of sport and I had to find my own way. Being positive and rising to the challenges that would lie before me, I felt, would define me not only as a player but also as a person.

The longer I spend in football, the greater awareness I've developed of how important the mind is both on and off the pitch. I've learned that the mind is like a muscle because it needs regular exercise in order to stay focused, confident, motivated and happy. Like most things in life, nothing worthwhile is achieved without work. Only when I've been exposed to tough times have I really started to understand my own psychology.

I found that as you progress up the leagues and get older, mental weaknesses come to centre stage and there is nowhere to hide from them. It is easy to think that you can brush them aside and treat them as if they don't exist. This can often work for a short period, I've found, but the things you are scared of come back even stronger, especially as matches and performances become more importance and more intense.

As you go up the football leagues, games become more intense and at times it feels like you are walking a tightrope. There are times when you wobble and make mistakes on and off the pitch, which is a normal part of life and sport. But what has challenged me is being able to regain my composure quickly when something doesn't go to plan.

Spending many years at Sporting Lisbon made winning games look like a formality. Perhaps this is why I never really questioned myself or had to really face losing and deal with it. When my team usually wins, I find it mentally tougher to deal with a loss or a draw; the thought of negative results beforehand very rarely enters your mind. You never heard that the manager was under pressure at Sporting Lisbon, because the team would win almost every week.

Mistakes and the fear of loss form a new pressure that has come into my life more recently, forcing me to question my identity. I think my fear of making mistakes has come from this desire and the hunger to do everything right when you get on the ball. When it doesn't go your way you start to question and over-analyse the reasons behind this and in my case you end up trying too hard.

Working with a sport psychologist, like Sam Kotadia, has made me realise that it is normal to fear making mistakes and important to make them part of your life. When I accept this and see that making mistakes is natural it removes some of the pressure I place on myself.

Today I treat each defeat or loss as a big learning opportunity. I look at why I lose and think critically about why I lost or didn't play well. I have now learned to make loss my friend and respect the losses. I've had to develop this mindset because I'm not the best player in the world and naturally regular losses are part of my career.

Since the age of 12 or 13 Ronaldo has not been able to accept defeat, as I recall. That word for him does not exist. Around this time I challenged Ronaldo by saying I was quicker than him, and as he could not accept this, we set up a challenge. We agreed to count to three and then start running. I remember our friend Fabio counted for us, and on 'two' I was already running and I won the race. Was it because I started running before him? In any case, he would not accept that I won and insisted we run again, until he proved he is the best or in this case the fastest. This mentality has served him well, from such a young age. I don't have his natural talent so I've never had the luxury of not accepting loss!

What puts him on top is the blessing of his natural talent, combined with this mentality of fighting and battling to get to the top. When Lionel Messi had won World Player of the Year four times, Ronaldo's belief that he could still dislodge him and prove he is the best in the world took real mental strength and conviction. We have a lot of examples of world-class players, such as Zlatan Ibrahimović, who is playing for one of the best clubs in the world, and who is in the elite crop of top players and paid accordingly. But it seems to me the difference between Ronaldo and some of the other world's elite is that he wants to be the best of the best. This comes from the mentality he and I have grown up with from a young age. The will to get right to the top is a weapon which very few people have in their armoury. Not having the natural talent of Ronaldo, I've had to ensure that I can deal with losses and setbacks on a regular basis. I knew in my heart this would improve my game.

Where's my identity?

From a young age I've always had the will-power and self-motivation to get up and go again when I'm being tested by life. This I know will always be with me and for some people never giving up is in their blood. This has led me to seeing how important the mind is in everything we do. Without motivation and confidence, very little would be achieved in my life. However, I felt there was more I could harness from the world of psychology, especially in relation to strengthening my overall identity on and off the football pitch.

Being true to myself is central to having a strong personal identity. When I have a strong sense of self my head is held high and I feel resourceful in the face of setbacks. I want to stand strong in the face of whatever is thrown in my direction. And when am I being true to myself? It is when I live life and play football without any inhibitions and complete freedom. On the pitch I play without boundaries, lose complete touch with time and find a sense of flow and connection with the game.

My main goal in developing my inner game was always to strengthen my identity on the football pitch. Having been exposed to loss in more hostile environments I had to develop my mental toughness. I know that when I'm playing football with my identity on full display I perform better and, most importantly, I enjoy my football so much more.

Around the time of moving to the UK to play for Charlton Athletic I had reached a point where I knew I could get more from my game if I could unlock more from my mind and deal with challenging environments more constructively. I clearly recognised that my lack of identity on the football pitch was holding me back and that it was born from having to stay positive in much harsher environments compared to the comforts of Sporting Lisbon. The key to achieving this, I believed, centred on overcoming the fear of making mistakes and rediscovering the innocence and freedom to play without any inhibitions, as I did without thinking in Lisbon. I always know that whatever I do in life, so long as it is authentic I will reap the rewards.

Naturally with age, my football life has become more serious and stopped me from playing with the complete freedom that I had when growing up in Portugal. When you have a family to feed and you want to help your extended family as much as possible too, pressure naturally creeps in.

At times during my professional career I've played football in a way that was not true to myself. I've fallen prey to the expectations of others and been influenced by the fear of making mistakes. All of these pressures have challenged me and in all honesty these only became apparent to me in my mid-20s. When I'm playing without my true identity, without authenticity, I lack the creativity I know is mine. I play too safely, sit in my comfort zone and feel heavy when I'm on the pitch. In performance, I also second guess myself and doubts creep in. I often start to 'hide on the pitch' and mentally will the clock to get to full-time as quickly as possible.

Players are often told by people in and around the game that these are the best years of your life. On the face of it that's true, but when you are in a slump it is so hard to still enjoy the game with the same amount of freedom and passion. There is no worse feeling than reflecting on a poor performance knowing that you could have played so much better. I want to look back on my career with no regrets, knowing that I left no stone unturned in my quest to be the best I could be and to get everything I could out of my life's passion.

Mental barriers

The fear of making mistakes at certain times in my career has prevented me from playing to my full capacity. Throughout my career I think that this has stopped me from being myself. What I've come to realise now is that mistakes are inevitable in all walks of life. You cannot hide from them.

After making a mistake or starting poorly in a game I find it harder to play with fluency. My reflex action is to start thinking more about the game in hand and consequently I lose my natural rhythm. Although my primary job is geared up to defend, when I'm analysing the game too much in my head I can be over-safe. Watching plenty of football over the years, I see that the great players are able to take risks and play without fear. Risks and gambles on the football field become defining moments for many of the great players. The most prominent risk both Ronaldo and I took at a young age was to leave our home and go it alone. This was the biggest choice we had to make in our lives, probably. It would have been easy to choose not to go, because naturally for a young boy it is scary. My mum never told me I had to go, or that I had to stay. She always said it was my choice. At the back of my mind I knew that whenever I returned home I would come back a man. Ronaldo and I both took that risk and because of it we are better people, and both able to continue supporting our families. I remind myself that if I'm able to make bold decisions like this in life, being myself on the football field should be a walk in the park!

Growing older, especially in a career where you have a short shelf-life, makes you more aware of the games that you could have played, but missed. With age, you start seeing your playing career as finite which adds more pressure on you to make sure you play your best in each game. I guess when you're young you are less conscious of making the most of every competitive game. This is why I've always been so motivated to squeeze every inch of talent out of myself, which led me to delving deeper into my inner game.

I asked and I received

It was during the 2009/2010 season at Charlton Athletic that I felt I needed someone to help me professionally with my mental game. My feeling was that I was getting too tight and over-thinking my game and consequently it felt like I was losing my identity. I needed someone to help me manage loss and disappointment so that in the face of defeat I could bounce back quickly. Despite having the DNA of a true warrior I needed direction to ensure that any form of loss would be shrugged off very quickly.

Luckily for me the manager at the time, Phil Parkinson, saw that I was carrying a heavy mind and would benefit from working on my psychology. Call it coincidence, or a profound intervention, the fact is that for a whole month I prayed every day for someone to come into my life to help me with my psychology. I remember the day that Phil Parkinson introduced me to Sam Kotadia. Phil told me that he had 'a good guy who can help you with the psychological part of the game'. He explained how they had worked together for many years and had proven time and time again that getting your psychology right makes the difference between winning and losing.

Sam came into my life at a point where I was in a team that was not winning every game, and consequently there was often tension in the dressing room with a manager under pressure. It's hard to say, but before I had Sam's help I would go deeper and deeper into myself and find it hard to be authentic and play my best football on the pitch. At this time there was a group of foreign players in my generation within the club. As a foreign player, you generally get closer and more friendly with the other foreign players and follow their careers. Some of them have now drifted out of the football leagues and maybe without Sam's support I might have done so too. But today I'm in the market, playing in one of the best leagues in Europe and I'm playing regularly.

When I started working on my mental game I could never have predicted the profound effect it would have on my performance or how it would influence my outlook on sport and life as a whole. But the journey was so important it has taken me along the path of gathering my thoughts in the form of this book.

It was clear that Phil Parkinson understood the importance of psychology in sport. His attention to detail is one of the best in the game and he knows the importance of making everyone in the team feel valued. Having been a player too, he understands what it means to fight and to work hard on the football pitch. Parky appears to have a similar mentality as Ronaldo and I have. We have a fire and a hunger to be the best we can be every day and always maintain a close attention to detail in all areas of the game.

Phil Parkinson's eyes can see inside you. I never went to him and asked for help with my mental game; he just knew. He is a master at the art of tuning into his players and getting the best out of them. Some managers will devote all their attention to the starting eleven and often neglect the fringe players. Parky at his best wouldn't let this happen. I've vowed to myself that if I ever become a football manager I will make sure my own attention and focus is not only on the eleven who are playing on Saturday, but on everyone in the squad. This is for many reasons, but mainly because if you can maintain the self-esteem of the players on the side-lines, when you do need to call upon them (which you nearly always need to do at some point) they will give you so much more. I know this from experience.

It was a real eye-opener for me to see first-hand that how you feel before you perform is critical to how the game progresses. Parky makes sure that he speaks to every player, knowing what to say to them and how. These interactions may only last a few minutes but are enough to get you feeling good and ready for action. It is now something I try to do regularly as a player on the football pitch. Whether I'm given the Captain's armband or not, I always want to help get the best out of my team-mates. Working with Parky encouraged me to do more of this.

His recent success was taking League Two club Bradford City all the way to the League Cup Final, which is the first time a fourth-tier team in English football has achieved this. It was another reminder how important the mental approach is in the game. If you have a team of fit, confident and well organised footballers you always have a fighting chance of winning, irrespective of who your opponents are. I was fortunate to be at the Wembley final to support my friend and be a part of this amazing run.

It is testament to Parky's understanding of his players that he could see there was often something missing in my performances and in training when we worked together at Charlton. He knew that I had the physical attributes and technical skills to excel in my role as a midfielder and he felt that the only thing holding me back was myself. My challenges lay predominantly in my mind. Parky saw how I would lose my head when I made mistakes and how I would end up hiding on the football pitch to protect myself from being exposed again. Seeing this in my game he didn't hesitate to introduce me to Sam Kotadia who he knew could help me.

Sam had worked with Phil Parkinson for many years. They combined at Colchester United and the club won a historic promotion to the Championship Division. Working with both the coaches and players, Sam helped build a culture that recognised the importance of Positive Psychology and what it takes to build a winning mentality within the team. At the time Colchester United had limited resources, but the club made up for this by paying extra attention to sport science, in particular sport psychology.

Often we had three-way sessions in which Phil Parkinson would outline what he felt the team needed from me. This then would give me and Sam more direction in our sessions to ensure that I delivered on his vision. It also placed a healthy and supportive pressure on me to deliver on Saturday.

The mind gym

As I've said before, the mind is like a muscle that needs regular exercise. Training with a sport psychologist is a full work-out for the brain! I remember after our first session coming away feeling lighter, more positive and, most importantly, more myself. The improvement in my feel-good factor was clear to others. The physiotherapist Nick Davis commented that it looked like a weight had been lifted off my shoulders. As our sessions progressed I recognised that this was an area of my professional game that needed attention. Throughout my career I've experienced times where negative psychology has damaged my performance and this was clearly helping.

Finding the right way to work

When you are working on something as personal as psychology, the way training is delivered is critical. Just as with physical training, much depends on the individual and the coach's ability to tune into their client and build a programme that is right for them. I had no real expectations of how Sam's support would help me, other than I wanted to overcome my fear of making mistakes and have a greater sense of freedom and confidence in my own abilities. Consequently I wanted to see the time invested with Sam result in stronger performances on the football pitch.

Very quickly we found a way to work, which we employ to this day. Once a month we spend the whole afternoon together. We work on problem-solving and we discuss mental strategies, ideas and techniques that I can use to develop my inner game on and off the pitch. For the rest of the month we talk several times on the phone before and after games, to see how the interventions I've put into place are working. Naturally, some are more effective than others. These regular conversations are critical to the fine-tuning of successful strategies. That constant feedback from experimenting and trying out new ideas and thinking strategies is where the real work happens. Putting what we discuss into practice is 80% of the work. The session brings in the ideas, but taking them and bringing them into the game is vital. Speaking regularly about what I need to do, where old poor habits are broken down and new healthy habits are established, helps make everything natural.

Sam told me he doesn't spend too long in preparing his sessions, so that he is able to think on his feet and truly listen to what I need. Like any professional, and footballers are no exception, if you over-think and over-prepare before and during matches, you lose your natural flow and it damages your expertise. This is relevant in our sessions: Sam trusts his expertise in such a way that he is not reliant on notes and any information he has to hand. Although he does bring materials on paper for me to look at and study, he doesn't let them dictate the flow of our conversations or the session as a whole. Sometimes they provide structure to the topics and areas we want to cover, but generally these come up naturally of their own accord.

Whatever we do in life, once we become expert we need to trust our instincts and automatic processes. If we don't trust them, and over-think what've got to do, the skill we have prac-tised for so long becomes laboured, as if we were learning the skill for the first time. Learning to trust without questioning is the only way to perform with class and authority. In the sessions I have with Sam this fortunately serves as a reminder that on the football field I don't need to think about what I'm doing. My instincts should be my only driver when I play.

Focus on feeling

Sam told me that the way in which a message is delivered is as important as the message itself, and in some cases more so. In order to put a mental technique into practise you need to fully commit to it and believe in what you are applying. As Sam has always said, part of the art of helping the client make this happen is to make the technique or principle come alive for them. This is helpful when talking with my team-mates to encourage them to play their best. It's also how Parky operates. He too focuses as much on how he delivers his coaching as on the words themselves.

Another of Sam's insights is that when we communicate, it's the feelings behind our words that carry most of the weight. This is one of the reasons why speaking with my friend Ronaldo gives me such a boost: it's not just about what we talk about but also the love and good-will that comes through.

From my experience of working with different coaches I've found that the ones who have a positive impact on their players are not necessarily the ones who have the best coaching methods but the ones who deliver their coaching with enthusiasm, desire and confidence. In some ways this is what you want your coach to pass on to you. When you are playing with these emotions, you find that the tactics, strategy and the overall game-plan fall naturally into place. If the coach can help me get into a positive state of mind, I'm always more likely to have the confidence to express myself on the football pitch and play fearlessly.

We continue to work together, Sam and I. Like any supportive relationship there are always new challenges and areas of improvement to discuss. To keep a professional relationship fresh after more than five years of working together requires something special.

Even in the modern game there remains a negative stigma attached to the use of psychology. When I first started to work with Sam, he rightly emphasised the importance of using sport psychology not only to fix problems, but to get better and to keep improving. Just as physiotherapists want to improve the body's conditioning and keep the body fit as opposed to treating physical injuries, sport psychologists want to improve and maintain a healthy mentality, rather than fix mental problems. It is much healthier to work on your psychology when you are feeling on top of your game. That way you are more likely to stay there.

Final thoughts

Complete success is impossible unless you can truly understand yourself. Having started my football career alongside the greatest footballer on earth and being nurtured by the great Sporting Lisbon Academy I got the taste of winning from an early age. It was only when I got thrown into the football leagues outside Sporting Lisbon that I was regularly exposed to the feeling of loss that comes with defeat. This is when I learned what it means to be positive and the importance of surrounding myself with good people in all areas of my life.

Magic reminders

- Playing football true to myself is behind all successful performances.
- Fear of making mistakes is the biggest cause of me hiding on the football pitch and not being myself.
- When I'm whole-heartedly committed to self-improvement I will always find the right people at the right time to help me on my journey.
- How you deliver your message when you are coaching and inspiring others is often more important than the words themselves.
- Surround yourself with people who have your best interests at heart, knowing you can call on them in times of need.

TWO

THE INNER BATTLE

When I feel comfortable in the presence of what I fear I always play football and live life with freedom.

I was the least talented in the Sporting Lisbon class of 1985. Developing my trade alongside Ronaldo meant that I had to develop a fierce work ethic to remain professional. There is no doubt about it, my life in sport has always been a battle and one that continues to push me to be positive and work hard in all circumstances.

A big portion of my ability to stay competitive has been down to mastering my inner game and learning to overcome the psychological pressures most professional athletes face.

This chapter talks about the inner enemies that I've learned to tame and manage over the years. In the world of football it doesn't take much for you get lost in the wilderness and stop making progress. No doubt, any of these inner challenges continue to have the power to derail my career if I become pre-occupied with them.

Dangerous goals

One of the challenges I've faced over the years is the desire constantly to set myself goals. Although setting regular goals works for some people, it takes me away from the present moment and blurs my overall day-to-day focus. There is no escaping the desire to want to perform well and as a professional athlete this means progressing up the leagues. Whatever your job, there is nearly always an ambition to progress in some shape or form. Some of the common goals for me include being picked for the starting eleven, playing in the Premiership, representing my country, and securing lucrative contracts in the game. These goals will always be present and, don't get me wrong, they're nice to achieve! But it is important that I don't become consumed by them. As this book describes, the only meaningful goal for me now is to *Win the Day* and allow any other successes to be natural by-products of this mindset.

During Sheffield Wednesday's promotion to the Championship everyone in the club was aware of the collective desire to win it. I was well aware that this would be an achievement to savour, but equally aware of the pressures that being pre-occupied with such a goal can bring. In order to navigate through the season in a fit and healthy state of mind, I knew it was important not to over-think and over-worry about the club's goal of winning promotion. My mentality had to stay focused on day-to-day events and what was within my control. Outcomes such as winning promotion are always out of the individual footballer's control.

My first years in football with Ronaldo certainly helped me to compete hard every day and avoid the desire to set too many ambitious goals in my mind. Being around someone with such an appetite for perfection made me dedicated to not getting too lost in the future and made me focus on the here-and-now. Moving away from this state of mind adds unhealthy pressure, and limits my ability to play with freedom. In the past, before using sport psychology principles, I would regularly imagine my footballing goals and ambitions. Playing in the best leagues in the world, playing for my country and winning the biggest tournaments in the game were common visions in my mind in the early years. It was only recently that I started to recognise that thinking too far ahead and indulging in visions of success was damaging to my game. Even allowing my mind to ruminate over whether or not I would be picked come Saturday was enough to disrupt my football. Frequently it resulted in me over-trying and pushing too hard on the football pitch. It created tightness in my game, resulting in me committing unnecessary fouls and regularly getting out of position and leaving the team exposed.

I can understand why many coaches suggest 'positive visualisation' to create positive states of mind and optimistic mindsets. By imagining positive pictures or reassuring voices, thus creating positive feelings, you are thought to be more likely to achieve your goals. This has never worked for me: it only created additional pressure. Suddenly I would need games to go a certain way in order for me to progress. Relying on positive visualisation falls down when unforeseen events arise, leaving me feeling helpless and demotivated because the inner vision didn't match up to reality. I would then lose my grip on the game and struggle to find the resources to get back into it.

Another aspect of visualisation which I found unhelpful was overly rehearsing past successes. In the past, after a top performance, the first thing I've wanted to do is to hold on to that taste of victory. This would often involve me reliving all of the great things I did in the game and how good they felt. But there is a danger in this. Over-rehearsing some of my recent and best performances places a greater pressure to perform well in the next game. You start to expect that a faultless performance and a win are in the bag.

When my mind has convinced me to expect another win next Saturday I play with less intensity, which works against me. If by luck it goes my way, the victory tastes less sweet because in my reality it was a foregone conclusion. The most nourishing and enjoyable victories are the unexpected ones that were born from turning up and giving 100% and feeling in control of my mind and body. This is probably true of successes in all walks of life. My advice is never to take anything for granted; I try to develop a mindful, moment-to-moment awareness of where I am and what I'm doing. There is more on this in Chapter 5 on mindfulness.

Laws of attraction

When I first came across Positive Psychology, many of the techniques I was introduced to described ideas like the 'law of attraction'. The law of attraction presents the notion that the longer you fixate on something in your mind the more likely you are to make it a reality. For example, believers in the law of attraction would say that if I see myself winning promotion to the Premiership with Sheffield Wednesday I'm more likely to make it happen. In my experience, life in sport very rarely goes the way I expect. No matter how regularly I imagine playing football to the level of Ronaldo, I will never be able to emulate him. This is why I stop myself from letting my imagination run too far. It can build unrealistic expectations.

Along the same vein of thought, outcomes and getting attached to positive and negative results are one of my biggest challenges. They stop me from being the best in any given moment. If I'm always imagining potential successes my actions in the present moment are weakened. I stop doing things with the care and attention they deserve and consequently whatever I'm doing suffers, whether I'm driving my car, eating, or playing football. In the same way, overly rehearsing visions of winning trophies and beating the opposition encourages me to start expecting to win and give less attention to my present focus.

Over-thinking about positive outcomes has left me feeling helpless in a game when things don't go to plan. I've found that I lack the flexibility to roll with the punches and consequently end up shocking the system. When my brain only imagines positives coming from the game I'm not toughening myself up for the potential negatives that could arise.

Certainly there are lessons here that can be applied to all walks of life. Getting attached to desired outcomes before achieving them can be damaging if, for whatever reason, you fall short. Then if you do manage to achieve the desired goal you enjoy the experience much more. Again although positive visualisation can create feelings of optimism, it can create unwanted pressure, encouraging me to take favourable outcomes for granted, and can leave me feeling demotivated and depressed if and when I'm unsuccessful.

I've also found that when your mind is indulging in all that you want to achieve you lose sight of all of the hard work that is required to get you there. You are more likely to forget that success does not grow on trees and often needs blood, sweat and tears to be achieved.

Talking of hard work, other than Ronaldo my other best friend in sport is the treadmill. This is the only time when I do allow myself to indulge my imagination!

Extreme emotions

In the football arena you are exposed to many extreme emotions: excitement, disappointment, happiness, sadness, pride and frustration are just a small handful. I've found that learning to keep a balanced mind and not getting moved by extreme emotions, whether positive or negative, is critical to my success. Taming extreme emotions is an inner battle that needs regularly to be fought and won. If not my game becomes rushed and uncontrolled, lacking the precision a Championship footballer requires. When my emotions start driving my game, the way the 90 minutes unfolds becomes very unpredictable.

Fear is one of the main emotions I've had to manage over the years to stay in the right mindset. Taming fear and overcoming any self-doubts is an inner battle that I've fortunately always won. When I do experience fear it feels like a fire has started in my brain and when negative thinking kicks in alongside this fire it grows out of control and damages my game. In the heat of a negative event fear causes the adrenaline to flow and it can get too much for me, making my whole body tight and slow to react. It is a bit like drinking too much coffee, where instead of making me alert in a positive way, it starts to work against me. This could happen when I'm not picked for the starting eleven on Saturday after expecting to be, or picking up an injury and being told you will be sidelined for a significant period of time. Worst is when I make a critical mistake out on the football pitch. All these have the capacity to trigger that rush of adrenaline in the brain and body.

Sam reminded me that this initial adrenaline response to setbacks will always be there to a certain degree. It was Sam who compared it to a fire in your brain: and the way you keep the negative fire burning is to fuel it with thoughts. Over-thinking and having an inner negative self-critic is like throwing wood onto the fire. The panic and inner discomfort last longer.

I've learned that the way to allow my mind and focus to move on from this experience of panic and fear is to know and respect that it is there, and just observe it until it burns out on its own. If I don't feed it with my negative thoughts, it burns out of its own accord and I return to peace. Keeping the lion inside of me controlled and in the right place works in my favour. It is when the lion and my fear start taking control of my game that I lose composure and play less well.

As the fans have pointed out, there have been times when I've tried to be in too many places on the football pitch and I start chasing the game. This is the tell-tale sign that fear has got the better of me and I'm being led by emotions. In this example fear has drawn out my fight instinct and encouraged me to try and be everywhere at once. Although I've always had the best interests of the team at heart, it's very rarely worked out in my favour.

Stepping out

Talking about the fear response, Sam explained how fear is hard-wired into our brains and is built in to stop us from taking unnecessary risks and protect us from danger. When our bodies think we are in danger the brain has an inner alarm that alerts us. This is often felt by an adrenaline rush, which results in either a fight or flight response. Big games, conceding goals, angry fans, despondent managers, and disagreements with the referees have all at some point got my fear response kicking in. Either way, when I let this natural fear response get hold of my game I lose control and composure. Being governed by fear can mean I play an overly safe game, or an overly reckless one.

Certainly what I've learned of late is that if I refuse to take healthy risks and put myself in scary situations I find it hard to progress in life and sport. I've learned that the brain has the capacity to grow and change and when we put ourselves into new and challenging situations our brain cells make new connections and establish new ways of working. When we do this our map of the world expands and we are capable of more. My thoughts about my game are not always a realistic picture of what is actually possible. Some psychologists say we become what we practise, and there is some truth in this. I've certainly found this in my professional career in terms of the way I play on the football pitch. Naturally you gravitate towards the things that feel safe, and the actions that feel safe are the ones that we rehearse the most.

I often get an instinct about what I should do in a game. Although my main focus will always be defensively minded, on occasions my instincts about what I can do can be quite daring. It may involve taking on players, getting into offensive positions, or attempting something new on the football pitch. When I've let my instincts guide me, I've created inspired performances. When the fear response kicks in and tells the brain 'you can't do that, if you make a mistake you will let down yourself and your team-mates'.

I have to keep reminding myself of this, especially in the role I play as a defensive midfielder. My job is primarily to play it safe, protect the ball, and help the team to rebuild their momentum. But I'm still capable of offensive play, scoring goals and assisting the strikers.

There have been times when I've stayed in my comfort zone and failed to take an opportunity for positive offensive play, and ended up playing it too safe. A prime example that I've seen on the videos of recent performances is when I'm in possession and space opens up in front of me. Instead of travelling with the ball and moving forwards, my immediate instinct (driven by my comfort zone) is to pass it.

Some of my best performances have proven to be when I'm able to venture forwards and be creative. Of course I need to make sure that this doesn't interfere with my primary defensive duties. Either way I can think of countless games where I've reaped rewards by stepping outside my usual map of the football pitch and explored the full territory. Naturally when you are being courageous and push outside of your comfort zone you will make mistakes. But the more you rehearse being bold in this way, mistakes become fewer and new challenges start to emerge.

One of the structured tasks Sam suggested to me was to try to touch the opposition's box as many times as possible when it was good to do so. Consequently this has led to creating, assisting in and scoring goals. I may have only scored two goals in the past couple of years, but both of them came from a desire to make something happen. I know for a fact that if I stay in my comfort zone then I will never grow as a person or as a player.

Back in the day when Ronaldo and I were partners in crime at Sporting Lisbon we always went the extra mile and pushed outside the comfort zone. The winning environment of Sporting Lisbon and being friends with the greatest footballer on earth in some ways gave me the platform to be daring and adventurous.

The challenging environment of English football was when comfort zones and playing a safer game became a more dominant consideration in my mind. When you play for Sporting Lisbon alongside Ronaldo, playing with complete freedom and passion is far easier and a given. When I have critical defensive responsibilities for my team extra safety and caution naturally become a core part of my game. Although I will never neglect my defensive duties it is important that I make all of my decisions with a clear mind and not as a knee-jerk reaction to feeling fearful. This gives me the freedom of mind to be daring and creative for the team at the right time. So there is certainly a place for fear in my game, as it reminds me to be vigilant of dangers on the football pitch.

Making fear your friend

Until I started working with Sam I never thought to label the fear I have inside me as a good thing. Now, when I feel that fear response, I'm able to sit with it without feeling uncomfortable. In my position as a defensive midfielder, I've learned to develop a deep respect for fear. As I've highlighted, being alert and sharp is vital to identifying dangers and get my positioning right. I try to be mindful of the fear, accept it and work with it. This means seeing the values and strengths that fear brings, but also the potential dangers.

So I've made fear my friend and in the process I'm able to use it to my advantage. If I enter the sporting arena without feeling fear, then it's likely that I'm not in the right state of mind to perform at my best; again everything for me is about balance. There have been many games where keeping this under control has been pretty difficult because it is easier said than done!

Mistakes

It was built into my mentality at a young age not to make mistakes. However, mistakes are an inevitable part of sport, even though they are seen as a formidable enemy by many professional athletes.

In so many areas of life we are conditioned to be afraid of making mistakes because immediately after making one you receive some form of criticism. As a child, this reprimand may come from a parent. In football this comes back to you from the fans, team-mates and the coaching staff. After making costly mistakes you can feel the tension on the training ground the following week. I can understand why I share the fear of making mistakes, especially as a defensive midfielder when one of my primary roles is not to lose the ball.

Not making mistakes became more of an issue when I moved away from Sporting Lisbon and had to play for league clubs and prove myself in highly competitive environments. One memory in particular sticks in my mind that reminds me how debilitating mistakes can be. It was at Charlton when I was playing under Alan Pardew. I played right-back for one game. Coming on at half-time against Ipswich when the team was losing 1–0, we ended up winning 2–1, and all of the goals came from my right-hand side. Playing with Darren Ambrose, I fed the ball into him several times which resulted in him setting up both goals. After this I really expected to start the next match, because I had shown I could come onto the pitch and change the game. The next game was away to Cardiff on the Friday and before it the manager called me to his office and told me that he had to play Chris Martin instead. It was so hard to take because I had trained well during the week with extra enthusiasm because of my contri- bution on the previous Saturday. Either way I accepted his decision and knew that I had to be ready because I was not far from being a regular for the first team.

On the day, it was like the previous game as I started in the second half against Cardiff. But two minutes later I had a red card. When Jay-Boothroyd passed to Michael Chopra (who was their striker) I was convinced that my defender had him covered, but he hadn't, and as I was the last man, I pulled his arm back. It was enough for Chopra to lose his balance, leaving the referee no choice but to send me off. This mistake was really hard to take, especially as I had been working so hard and feeling so positive about my football. It was a real blow. I was so close to getting into the first team and having to spend three matches away was tough.

Avoiding crucial mistakes is a vital component of winning football matches, and making mistakes is also an important part of getting better. Footballers never mean to make mistakes, but when they arise we cannot let them affect our state of mind, otherwise performances can quickly fall apart. Some of the greatest ever athletes attribute their success to making mistakes time and time again. Using mistakes as positive experiences and not negative ones helped them in so many ways to master their sport. But it's easier said than done, that's for sure.

I've noticed that when I'm not making mistakes it is usually because I'm not proactive in the game. The player analysis I've done over the years shows me that making a few mistakes here and there indicates that I'm playing a very active role in the game.

The fear of making mistakes is useful as it keeps my defensive duties in check, but what is more of a consideration for me is learning not to let the mistake disrupt the flow of my performance in any shape or form. A lot of what I've learned with Sam over the years has involved the management of mistakes and being able to bounce back quickly. If I lose the battle in dealing with mistakes constructively, although I always bounce back, it takes me a little longer and valuable playing time can be lost.

The pain of loss

Several months ago I learned that the brain likes to experience winning, but *hates* to lose. It was during a particularly interesting session with Sam where we spoke about how losing feels so much more painful than the equivalent high of winning a football match. This explains why the fear of losing and making mistakes can be so powerful at times. For example when someone gives something tasty to eat it is a positive experience, but if someone takes your meal away from you, the pain is much stronger than the enjoyment experienced when you received it. Beating your rivals in a local derby feels great, don't get me wrong, but the pain of losing to your rivals goes much deeper. Scoring a goal at a crucial time gives an amazing rush, but is no comparison to the pain of conceding an important goal at the last minute. The pain lingers on, often for days.

So it was a breakthrough to understand why losing was so painful in the sporting arena. It also explained why a team often becomes overly defensively towards the end of games when it's winning by a narrow lead. Despite the fact that the current strategy of playing offensively is working, we will often change what is proving to work. You now have your lead to protect, so your whole outlook on the match changes. The idea of losing such games when you are ahead in final minutes can be crippling at times. I've felt myself getting tight and starting to over-think when the team is protecting a tight lead.

Unfortunately this weakness is rooted in all of our minds and will always be there. But once we understand it, we can develop an awareness of the principle, giving us greater control. It certainly helps me to understand why and how my emotions and behaviour can change almost automatically.

People pressure

When you have a high status in football, the fans, the coaching staff, the club owners, and your team-mates have expectations that need to be met. Although I've always been quite self-contained and focused on only what I can control, the pressures and expectations of others can affect you in a negative way. It's another inner enemy that will always be present in professional sport and probably in many other walks of life. My work with Sam has helped me manage the expectations of those around me at the club. Knowing that there are things beyond my control helps me focus my efforts on the things that I can change.

My experience tells me that expectations can damage performance by encouraging you to become overly concerned about pleasing yourself and others. When the pressure of expectations kicks into my game, it can go in one of two different directions. Either I start to hide on the football pitch, taking fewer risks, or I will start trying too hard. Both are damaging to my game.

In such a high profile sport, it's really easy for a footballer's identity to get tied up in the people around them. Often players will want to read what is being said about them in the media. Worrying about what others think of you can encourage you to take your focus off your performance and instead battle with the goal of impressing others. Thinking about the expectations of others can also leave you feeling you have let people down when you don't perform to the highest standard. Fortunately it is not an inner enemy that has dominated too much of my life.

Having a strong relationship with the fans is very important to me. They see I always give 100% for the team, every time I step out onto the football pitch, and so long as they trust me to do that, I have their respect. This is what I think is important to them. Winning is obviously important too, but even when we lose there is still respect from the fans, which has helped reduce the pressure that I can sometimes put on myself to ensure that the team get favourable results. As long as I always give my all, I will be respected by my team-mates, the coaching staff and the fans.

There was such a great welcome for me at Sheffield Wednesday by everyone involved within the club that nothing gives me more pleasure than holding the stripes of Sheffield Wednesday high. I just need to be careful that my desire to please the fans does not get in the way of playing my best football. It's a balancing act.

When I first received the Captain's armband there was a danger this would make me put unhealthy pressure on me. But I've never become too attached to the armband, and always give of my best whether Captain or not, leading by example and putting myself on the line for the team. I always aim to help and support my team-mates, listening and talking to everyone around me. This will never change, whether I'm Captain or not.

With a little help from Ronaldo over the years I've managed to develop healthy expectations for myself. Working with him at Sporting Lisbon certainly set the benchmark of always giving 100% each day. In Ronaldo's case I don't think he has any real expectations other than to be the best he can be and to work hard every day. From this mindset the trophies and the success followed. There are very few people who can soak up the pressure he faces and make it work for him.

Ronaldo is the kind of player who can turn a negative experience into a positive one. He's a guy who shows this all of the time on the football pitch. When Rooney was sent off in the 2006 World Cup and Ronaldo was controversially involved, he knew he would be booed by the English fans when the new season began. But he seemed to use all of that energy to his advantage by harnessing it in a positive direction. His football has always done the talking, and because of his brilliance once again the fans came around and started cheering his performances. Ronaldo also had the challenging task of winning over the Spanish fans at Real Madrid. Real Madrid is an institution. It demands the highest level of football, so coming to a club like that you have to win over all of the stake-holders if you have the intention of staying for the long term. Ronaldo no doubt did this with flying colours, in the process breaking a handful of club records. It was the same at Sporting Lisbon, irrespective of any initial perceptions about him and his game he would always be able to get everyone on his side because of his footballing brilliance. In my own case, if some people don't like me, I accept it because I understand that that you can't please everyone. But Ronaldo is capable of getting everyone to like him. I think this stems from him having strong personal goals and values that prevent outside pressures from dislodging his focus on being successful. At Sporting Lisbon we developed high personal standards in all areas of the game which we could always rely on irrespective of any outside pressures.

Pleasing the decision makers

In the football arena, pleasing the manager and coaching staff is critical and unfortunately there is no escaping this. The opinions of managers influence the overall success of every footballer's career. I've noticed that there are times during training when the manager is present and the tempo of team's performance improves. You feel the team's overall desire to impress. This happened a lot under Dave Jones. Because he wasn't involved in the team's training all of the time the tempo would change when he arrived. Although I would always play to the same intensity irrespective of who was present at training, I can see how getting caught up in the need to impress the decision makers would damage my game. I'm already highly motivated and driven to work hard every day, so that any extra pressure to up my game would result in me trying too hard and not playing naturally.

Being aware of the importance of impressing the decision makers in the club centres on that all-important moment when you find out whether or not you are in the starting eleven for Saturday. There is always tense anticipation waiting to find out who is going to play. I still get butterflies as I know being picked or not is something outside of my control and often unpredictable. If I'm always thinking during the week about being picked for Saturday's game, I find myself getting tense. The strange thing is, when I'm not thinking about it, I improve my chances of being picked. Why is this? Maybe because when my mind and body are fighting to get in the starting eleven I always seem to make it harder for myself, letting unforced errors creep in and being unable to play a natural and relaxed game.

The uncontrollable nature of being picked is an unhealthy pre-occupation, and on reflection it has affected my performances in training. Irrespective of how happy I am with my performances, if I want to be picked on Saturday I know I have to keep my bosses happy. There have been times when this inescapable part of football has got in the way of me playing my natural game. The worst feeling is when you expect to start and you realise that you haven't been picked. This is where expectations can leave you feeling lost. My mentality of 'winning the day' has protected me from this over the years, but like many things this at times is easier said than done.

There is always uncertainty in football and at times it's very easy to get distracted by the unpredictability. I remember at the end of the 2012/2013 season when there was one year left on my contract, there was talk of me leaving the club. It was a very unsettling time for me, but my instincts told me to be faithful and loyal to the club. I know in my blood I was meant to play for Sheffield Wednesday, and I couldn't ignore what my instincts were saying. Despite the few doubters who thought I didn't have the ability or skill to play at the Championship level I knew I had to stay put. I worked hard to put all the speculation to the back of my mind. Irrespective of what the press, the fans and my coaching staff were saying about me, taking each day as it came with my strong work ethic meant I found a way to stay where I belonged – at Sheffield Wednesday.

The Madeira trip

An early memory of the power the key decision makers hold in the game takes me back to Sporting Lisbon. I remember Ronaldo played for the Under-16s for Sporting Lisbon when they were scheduled to play against his home town on the island of Madeira where he grew up. Naturally Ronaldo was expecting to be in the starting line-up. He was so excited because it was one of the first times all of his friends and family would be able to see him play.

I can't remember the exact details but just before the game Ronaldo and one of our friends did something out of line and they punished Ronaldo by not letting him play. On the Friday night we were getting ready to travel on Saturday in anticipation of playing on Sunday. When they announced the squad Ronaldo realised that his name wasn't there.

64 |

It was so painful for him, he was crying. He couldn't understand why they did that to him. They knew he wanted to go and see his mum and dad and his friends. I sat with him and said that if I was in the starting eleven I would go to the manager and tell him to take me off and put Ronaldo in my place; unfortunately this was not possible.

Despite this Ronaldo didn't lose his drive and his motivation. In his heart he knew he was the best even in the face of this setback. He had such a powerful mentality even back then. No one could control him or change his fate in the game. His mentality was and still is unmovable in my eyes. I think setbacks have made him stronger and an even scarier guy to face on the football pitch. I know he will continue to prove time and time again how great he is.

Hard to please

From a young age I've always pushed myself physically and mentally to be strong on and off the football pitch. Growing up with Ronaldo most certainly inspired me to always give 100%. During the season, most afternoons after training, I go straight to the gym and get on the treadmill. Without fail in the evenings I commit time to doing yoga and meditating. In the off-season I don't let up. When I return to Portugal to spend time with my family I often hire a personal trainer to ensure I stay physically fit. I do everything I can to push myself.

Sometimes this hunger can overspill into trying too hard and being too conscientious. When you have high personal expectations and standards it is very easy to let them interfere with your natural game. It has happened to me many times before.

I have always put extra pressure on myself to reach a certain standard in the game. I believe I can play in the Premiership comfortably. I think all footballers at our level feel confident playing football to the highest level and I'm not alone in this. As far as I'm concerned I need to make sure I don't put too much pressure on myself to reach this level. As I've demonstrated, I'm already highly motivated and naturally a fighter and any more pressure will overspill into trying too hard on the football pitch. I have to put these larger goals and expectations aside and not lose track of day-to-day actions and processes.

Being thrown a curve-ball

The ups and downs in the sporting arena can be physically and mentally exhausting. There is constant change which is a challenge in itself. Players come and go from the club, the coaching staff change, there are constant alterations to fixture lists and match-day tactics. Irrespective of how well I'm prepared for a match there will always be events in football that arrive uninvited.

Being flexible in my preparation is important, so that if something changes right at the last minute I can adjust accordingly. Trying to prepare for every eventuality is tiring; you can't run through all potential outcomes trying to predict what may or may not happen. What I can control are my reactions to unforeseen events. Even during times when negative events strike and it feels like I automatically start feeling despondent I know I've a choice how to react (however difficult this may be).

Some of the hard, uncontrollable events in football that I've had to manage include having to deal with the frustration of getting injured, not been selected by the manager due to their personal preferences, and being sent off or booked unfairly by the referees. Without mental toughness, I would have found it a real challenge to recover from some of my experiences at Sheffield Wednesday. For several periods since Sheffield has been in the Championship, I've found myself side-lined and out of the action. This is always the worst place to be as you are completely helpless; it is incredibly frustrating at times. It is even harder when you feel you are there for no real fault of your own.

Most players find it easy to feel positive when things are going well, but when you are thrown bad luck this is when you really find out how strong your psychology is. You cannot escape the reality that there will be tough times. What I've learned with the nature of emotions and the human mind is that it is impossible to feel positive all of the time. When you are struck down by bad luck it helps to be accepting of the circumstance and not fight any of the emotions that arrive, however negative they may be. When I try to push back at what has happened I end up creating more stress.

When it has not been going my way, the tendency is to think that the world is against you. When I feel like the victim it becomes even harder to improve on the football pitch. I believe that in all walks of life you have to take ownership of your behaviour and your actions, otherwise you will never be in control of your career. There have been times when my mind has gone down this path. There is no doubt that this thinking leaves you feeling low in confidence and lacking the motivation to give of your best.

The problem with the understandable pain and sense of loss when I'm dealt a bad hand in football is my immediate response to rebel against what has just happened. Usually this is an internal battle with my thoughts. I get caught up in negative cycles of thinking, trying to understand what has just happened and what I need to do to improve the situation. I found this incredibly damaging to my state of mind, especially when there is nothing you can do about it. The negative thinking can be so overwhelming that there have been times when sleeping felt like the only way to escape it.

I understand why I battle against pain when it arises, even when it is outside of my control. In my head I think that I'm able to escape it by over-thinking about what has just happened. It is a knee-jerk reaction for me. I believe I can think myself out of trouble, as opposed to the more healthy response of letting go and surrendering to events.

Injuries and suspensions are two prime examples of when my mind tries to get on top of the situation in hand but in reality I just have to ride it out. Battling against uncontrollable circumstances makes it so difficult to start playing good football after time on the side-lines.

Challenges outside of my control were thrown at me the moment that I entered the world of football. I remember Ronaldo and I having to look out for each other and having to be vigilant from the first moment we arrived at Sporting Lisbon. With high levels of crime in the city and being envied for being a footballer there were dangers at every turn. Whenever Ronaldo and I travelled by train around the city, we always had to protect ourselves from people trying to steal our wallets. There was even a time when we were both held at knife-point. We both stood our ground and fortunately the offenders retreated.

News of Ronaldo's footballing prowess started to reach the newspapers when he was still young and this made it difficult for him at school, because the other kids were jealous and would often try to beat him up. It got so bad that he had to be moved to a new school. Just because he was Ronaldo and he was famous, other students wanted to fight with him. But when he moved to his new school and the other students found out that Ronaldo had arrived, the same thing happened. Its remarkable how all of this, if anything, made him stronger.

Dark times

Injuries are by far the worst nightmare for an athlete. Within the blink of an eye, your whole professional life can suddenly change. But every athlete will suffer injury, and battling with the negative emotions involved is a skill we all have to learn.

Kelly Youga played at Charlton Athletic with me several years ago. He was an incredibly talented and ferocious left-back who was playing some of the best football of his career. Everything was looking good for him. During the first half of an uneventful mid-week game against Bristol Rovers in League One, I remember Kelly going in for a 50/50 challenge while the ball was high in the air. Unfortunately Kelly came out of the tackle badly and he found his knee took the full brunt of his opponent's right foot.

He was side-lined for the rest of the season with ligament damage to his knee. Within a second his career took a serious dip. Since then it has taken him the best part of three years to start playing competitively again. Strangely, you see serious injuries happen to other players and for some reason you never imagine that the same thing could happen to you.

You cannot predict events like these and in all honesty you can never really prepare for them. Emotionally you cannot be sure how you will react. Battling against your circum-stances is a natural reaction and although it is not helpful in times like this, thinking that you won't be caught up in them at all is wishful thinking. When you are hit by something like this the best way to deal with it is just to do as little as possible. When the only remedy is time, shutting down and going with the flow, however hard, is where to aim. In my experience, this is easier said than done.

When I fractured my ankle in February 2014 my world at that time came crashing down. In the beginning I found it impossible to keep negative thinking at bay, battling in my mind with what had just happened with almost complete disbelief. I had to surrender to the negativity and ride through it. Trying to suppress, and fight with it in my mind, didn't work for me. No matter how positive you are, when something like this happens there is no escaping feeling negative. In situations like this the best course is more about damage limitation and learning to accept what has just happened.

Although it was obviously a very difficult time for me, I managed to stay focused and take each day as it came. This is where my mentality of winning the day came into its own. I would never look too far into the future and tried to stay focused on being the best I could be each day. It made me realise that there were positive actions and steps I could take that gave me some control over my own wellbeing and the world around me. My daily practice of focusing very intently on everything that was within my control gave me the mental toughness to ride through this setback and get back to training quicker than anyone expected. There is much more on winning the day, and on the practice of mindfulness, later in the book.

Coming down

All of the 90-minute performances I've been involved in have created the full range of emotions within me – excitement, frustration, disappointment, pride, pain, happiness and sadness – the full works. However strongly or however many of these emotions I experience during a game, one thing for sure is that adrenaline will be coursing through my body.

Once the 90 minutes are over, coming down from the chemical high of any performance is a challenge. Naturally as an athlete you want to keep that winning buzz going, or find a way to work off your sorrows after a poor performance.

When the match is over I have to be disciplined not to over-think the performance irrespective of whether it was good or bad, and come down off the emotional rush of the game. When I'm pre-occupied with the previous match it takes me away from the here-and-now and stops me being my best come Monday. Trying to keep that high going or escape the pain of bad performance by over-thinking can leave me feeling mentally exhausted and drained when I train at the beginning of the week. Consequently training at the right intensity becomes much harder.

If I have mid-week games, coming down gently becomes even more important. Being able to detach after the game, irrespective of the result, and regroup quickly for the next challenge is critical. When the fixtures are coming thick and fast I try hard not to get sucked into an emotional spin.

After any performance, re-grounding yourself is an important process, and I learned that the hard way. In January 2014 we beat Leeds 6–0, arguably the best result of the year for the team and naturally we were on a high. My close friend Miguel Llera also played in our great win. The whole team was determined to continue this good feeling.

Miguel and I didn't let ourselves come down and we started planning a New Year's meal for our families, busy discussing what champagne we would have with our meal, with the expectation of winning the next game which was away at Bournemouth. I remember saying to Miguel that 'we'll win the next game, no problem'. But the next Saturday the game didn't start as planned, and we ended up losing the game convincingly. It was one of the worst games of the season, and I was so disappointed with my performance I went up to the club office and told them not to pay my wages that week. It was a wake-up call in the importance of managing success correctly. Over the years I've learned how to manage setbacks and defeats but at times I've failed to treat successes with the respect they deserve.

Piecing together what went wrong, what happened was that I didn't give myself time to come down from this great victory. My mind had drifted to the outcome of winning the next game because of a natural desire to keep the emotional high going. I was living in a fantasy world throughout the whole week, pre-planning our celebrations in the evening with our families. As I've said, some coaches and psychologists recommend rehearsing the emotional highs of past victories to get fired up for the next game. For me this is a dangerous distraction. It takes my mind off my key match processes and actions, and makes me feel out of control when things do not go to plan during the match. Predictably during the week my training failed to have the usual attention to detail because my focus was on the future and not on the present moment. I had already won the next game in my mind.

My coming-down routines are critical to ensure my mind doesn't drift to over-thinking about the past, good or bad. It is a constant challenge and something I do battle with frequently. The emotional rush of a game is addictive, encouraging you to find ways to keep the rush going. Whether or not my emotions are good or bad I need to find ways to vent them and switch off. When Ronaldo is feeling heavy and needs to come down, he told me that he likes to swim for an hour. This helps him to drop any frustrations and leave the pool feeling fresh and light. He told me how time flies for him when he's swimming. One hour of swimming feels like 20 minutes and afterwards he feels like he wants to fly. After stepping out of the pool he is like a 15-year-old again, full of energy and motivation. Every week I take my kids swimming and remind myself of the benefits of getting away from it all in a healthy way.

Final thoughts

Inner battles and challenges are always present in life as in sport. Despite what it may look like to an outsider, I've realised that whatever level you are at in the game there are common challenges all athletes face, whether you are playing for Real Madrid or Sheffield Wednesday. None of us is immune from having to battle with tough times in our own world. Over the years I've developed a keener awareness of what has the capacity to damage my happiness and my overall success in the game.

Magic reminders

- After 90 minutes of football I have to be disciplined to not over-think the performance irrespective of whether it was good or bad. I need to come down off the emotional rush of the game and encourage my mind to focus away from football.
- When I'm injured the best way to deal with it is just to do as little as possible. When the only remedy is time, shutting down and going with the flow, however hard, is what I need to focus on.
- When I've something to prove on the football pitch I start to feel tight and fail to play to my full potential.
- The brain likes to experience winning, but *hates* to lose.

Losing football matches seem more painful than the equivalent high of winning matches.

- One of the worst feelings in football is when I expect to be in the starting eleven and I realise that I haven't been picked. This is where expectations have left me feeling completely dejected.

- Although not making mistakes is a critical component of winning football matches, I've learned that making mistakes is also an important part of improving as a person and as a player.

THREE

THE ENGINE ROOM

How I feel is the biggest predictor of how I perform.

The last chapter was about all those inner challenges which are ever present for me, and probably for most people in sport and other walks of life. Being able to manage them and not let them define me makes the difference between winning and losing. How I react to life's challenges is what I feel will determine overall success in the game.

My engine room is what I see as my mental and physical headquarters. Its primary duty is ensuring I've plenty in the tank to deal with whatever life and sport throws at me. This chapter talks about the collection of principles and mindsets that help me to win my inner battles and stay positive. Drawn from a lifetime of experience, from childhood days and when I grew up with Ronaldo to my recent work on my psychological game, I talk about how I keep myself feeling resourceful and in a balanced state of mind.

Firing on all cylinders

The first and most important principle of my engine room is to make sure that before any performance I'm in a resourceful state of mind. The arena of professional sport constantly changes and every day there are new challenges, so my emotions are in a regular state of flux. Learning how to control and manage my state of mind has been a critical part of my training regime over the last few years. In the past, my emotions would often take the lead role in how my performance went. If I was fortunate enough to be feeling good then I was more likely to have a good game, but if I went to games feeling unconfident and nervous the opposite was true. Being able to stay on top of my state of mind in whatever circumstance on the football pitch has helped me in so many ways.

I've found playing well, for me, depends on feeling good, by which I mean that in a balanced state of mind: not too adrenaline-fuelled, not too relaxed. Staying aware of my emotions stops me getting lost in them and losing control. I remind myself that overly positive emotions can be as damaging as negative ones. Once I start to dwell on a positive experience, attachments can be formed and consequently peace of mind and mental balance are lost. There is nothing wrong in me savouring positive feelings, events and experiences, I just need to keep the flow by not attaching to them.

The constant up and down of emotions in the football arena are unavoidable. Some of the times when my emotions are on the edge include finding out what team the manager has selected, when we have a short period of time left in the game to protect a lead, when I make a mistake, when the whistle blows after 90 minutes irrespective of the result, or if I receive direct criticism from a coach or a team-mate. The key way I'm able keep my state of mind balanced is to step outside of my emotions and look at them from afar. It is a bit like watching myself on a TV screen as opposed to being inside of my head and it stops my emotions dictating my next actions on the football pitch. It gives me a moment to gain some clarity on the situation and make better decisions. If I can maintain a clear awareness of my emotional state I naturally find peace. It is when I battle with my emotions or when I let them guide my actions that my state of mind suffers and performance drops. Standing back and observing my state of mind, rather than letting it overwhelm me, is part of mindfulness, and there is more about this in Chapter 5.

Whatever my feelings are at any given moment, good or bad, I now know that if I leave them alone my mind and body return to a state of calm. The image I have in my mind is of throwing a stone into a still lake. The stone is like my thoughts, creating ripples in my mind. When I leave the thoughts alone without getting caught up in them, the lake naturally returns to stillness.

The sweet spot

Controlling arousal levels is the key to finding a balanced and productive state of mind. When my emotions are over-aroused – by being extra excited, nervous, or too determined to get a positive result – I play badly. What happens is that I make poor decisions, get booked for late fouls, fatigue quicker and lose my sharpness. When I'm over-aroused, my mind is busy and everything feels like it is in a rush. It constantly feels like I'm running out of time and I'm up against it.

At the other extreme, when under-aroused I lack the right, higher intensity to compete, and find it hard to rise to the challenge. I am slow to react, I compete with less conviction and my work-rate is much lower.

The art is to find the middle point between being under and over-aroused. When I hit this sweet spot everything feels effortless. When I find this spot it feels like I'm in the zone and totally at peace with my game. I feel light and at times it feels like I know what to do even before the ball has come to me.

As I explain shortly I can call on a range of techniques and mindsets to help me find this sweet spot. I carry them everywhere with me now. Because my natural state is on the anxious side, my tool-box contains tools to pull me in the other direction by removing some of the pressure I've also put on myself. These are all described in the second part of this chapter.

The butterfly point

Sam introduced me to the work of Positive Psychologist Michael Neil. In relation to arousal levels, he talks about a principle called the butterfly point. Imagine a butterfly flying around within your immediate reach and your goal is to hold the butterfly in your hands without doing it any harm. Once your hands have surrounded the butterfly, it is important that you don't squeeze your fingers together too tightly because you might crush the butterfly and if your grip is too light, the butterfly will escape. As with so many things, the idea is to find the right balance.

Being overly driven and motivated to be successful in football is part of my natural state. This hunger is not necessarily a bad thing: but there are times when it can spill over into trying too hard. The danger is that before games I can overthink and over-analyse because of my desire to be the best I can be, which can lead me to feeling uptight and anxious on the football pitch. There have been times when I've given away unnecessary fouls, tried to be everywhere at once, made rash decisions because I thought there was less time to react than there actually was, and made wayward passes because of being too hungry and too eager.

Once when I was working under Phil Parkinson we were playing Swindon in the play-offs and it was a critical game.

My heart was racing and consequently I was really keen to do everything possible to help us win the game. It was such an amazing atmosphere, with the game being televised too, so the build-up around the match was intense. The potential to travel to Wembley and play Derby in a big play-off final was exciting. The whole team had a sense of belief that we could achieve this. This is where Parky comes into his own: getting the team mentally ready for big games is one of his best attributes.

Unfortunately we didn't win the game. Sam gave me his thoughts on the game and he felt that I was trying to be everywhere at once, trying to do too much and consequently losing some of my control in the game. This was a time when my heart was racing and my inner lion took control. Over the years this is where Sam has become a critical part of my game. He has helped me to keep my arousal levels in check and not to let my heart and my emotions take over.

There is no doubt that when I've played well on so many occasions it's because of being able to control my arousal levels and not let the adrenaline take over. This is what Phil Parkinson did so well alongside his work with Sam. He knew what to say to each player to help them find their right state of mind. Players who were naturally a little lazy at times would receive a more authoritative line of coaching, while for those who tried too hard and often got anxious, a more relaxed approach worked.

Once my belief was that when you are up against it you need to double your efforts and try harder. On reflection I now realise that the harder you try to get what you want, the further away you can push it. Again, finding that middle point between under and over-trying is when I find my flow and get the just rewards.

High heart rate

Over-arousal from emotions affects my body as well as my mind. When my heart rate is elevated I'm more likely to think that I have to take action quickly, even if we are talking about a split second. It's a bit like over-revving your engine and not getting the productivity out of it. There have been many times on the football pitch when a racing heart-rate meant I haven't composed myself and consequently made a poor pass or tackle because I didn't have a clear mind to assess what was going on around me. This is another example of how when my emotional state is not balanced my performance suffers.

In the past I've worked with coaches who have got me to try harder and focus harder when I'm not playing well. This doesn't work for me and it ends up pushing my heart-rate up even higher, forcing me to lose any composure and any control I had on the football pitch. A calm and controlled pulse rate is usually a sign of well-centred arousal levels and a calm mind that is properly anchored to what I'm doing at the moment.

Emotions spread

Football is not a solitary sport: everything you do affects other players. On the pitch, emotions and states of mind spread from player to player, person to person. When other players around you have negative mindsets it's very easy to start carrying around their baggage too. This always used to happen to me and naturally my performance would follow the negative mood of the team. It's very common when a team is on a losing streak. Negative thinking can spread like wildfire within a team. When players are negative around you, it puts extra pressure on you when you have the ball. You don't quite get the level of support you usually would and it becomes harder to play correctly. If one of your team-mates is hiding on the football pitch, perhaps because they don't feel confident, you can make the mistake of trying to cover for them. Consequently, the team can end up losing their shape because of trying to compensate for a team-mate's negativity. This is where I have to return to focusing on what is within my control and learn to keep my emotional distance. If I allow the emotions of other players to affect my thinking, I'm in a vulnerable position. It is incredibly important that you are able to stay composed and focused when a significant proportion of your team-mates are feeling bad.

Spreading the love

Since working on my own identity and inner strength, I have not only kept my own state of mind strong, I have also been able to pull my team-mates out of their own negative thinking. But it is important to focus on my own state of mind primarily: when I think too hard about the ways my team-mates are playing I lose focus on myself and what I should be doing as a player. When my focus is on me, I naturally support myself and my team-mates without difficulty, each in their own way.

I need to speak to some of my team-mates nice and calmly, while others need a firmer approach. Everybody is different, and certainly one size doesn't fit all in terms of psychology. In 2012 at Sheffield Wednesday, when we were in League One, I was talking with Jermaine Johnson during a game. In my eyes he was the one with the capacity to win us games so it was always vitally important for the team to keep him in a positive state of mind. Then Gary Megson shouted at him from the touch-line and I could see Jermaine slowly lose his head and focus. I knew the team needed him so I started to talk with him nice and calmly and I said, 'I need you, you are the best player, you are the one who can get us the three points'. It made him feel very important, which he was, and as a result of this conversation I believe he stepped up and won us the game. The conversation helped him come back to the game and not get lost in negative thinking and emotions.

Finding the right state of mind

When my emotions are not balanced, what I do in all parts of my life suffers. I try to be aware of my state of mind as often as possible: it is so important in everything that I do. The rest of this chapter describes tools in my toolkit which help me keep my emotions in check. They stop anxiety and excitement getting the better of me. They include deep breathing, playing down the importance of events, imagining the worst, acceptance and finding silence. These are all tools which can help everyone stay in the right state of mind to achieve success in all aspects of life.

Stopping to breathe

Deep breathing has been a rock for me in helping me to find a balanced and calm state of mind. I have a simple routine when I practise deep breathing. I sit or stand comfortably and allow my mind to focus on my breathing. I breathe deeply through my nose and out through my mouth. I make sure my focus is aware of the rising and the falling of each breath. To make sure that my mind stays in the right place, I count each rise and fall so that my thinking is solely on my breathing. Sometimes I can give myself a number of deep breaths to reach in order to focus.

I carry this technique everywhere with me. Ideally I will be seated when I do this, but it works wherever I happen to be. Standing in the middle of the football pitch, watching the match from the bench, wherever I am I can always rely on this. It is ideal when I feel the need to regain my composure, perhaps when I've been given the bad news that I'm not in the starting eleven, or out on the pitch when we have conceded a goal.

Deep breathing helps me lose any tensions that I may be carrying. It pulls me back to the present immediately. I remember our first year in the Championship Division when we played Peterborough at home and we won 2–1. It was a game where I cannot remember making a single mistake, which is rare. Deep breathing played centre stage in this performance because throughout the 90 minutes I was present and aware of everything that was going on around me. In nearly every game in the Championship you have to deal with a constant barrage of curve-balls that come your way, and deep breathing on this occasion helped me to weather any mini-storms during the 90 minutes.

I think Ronaldo also uses deep breathing to ground him at key moments. I'd imagine that it helps him to be present and focused to execute. Although he's never told me this, I believe he takes a moment to get clarity on where he is and what he needs to do. It's certainly a technique which has never failed me and it will always be one of the most effective ways to keep my game together, especially when I make a mistake on the football pitch.

Playing down the importance of the performance

Before important matches, to keep my state of mind composed, I often play down the importance. I say things to myself like, 'it's just another game', or 'I'm just having a kick-about' to soften the intensity. People do the same thing before important exams or a driving test: tell yourself it's just a practice session to help stay calm. By adopting a thinking strategy completely in opposition to my current state of mind of being fired-up, pumped-up, excited and nervous, my state-of-mind is pulled nicely into the middle. Obviously I know the game is important and that I will give 100% but I just use this to ensure I don't try too hard.

This technique is definitely reserved for big matches when everything is heightened. It has helped me to be composed a few times in big moments. When we won promotion to the Championship Division a few years ago, as we came closer and closer to the climax of the season each game felt more and more important. When you are on the verge of winning promotion suddenly everything you can normally do with your eyes closed on the football pitch becomes a challenge.

This is when this tool comes into its own for me. Under intense pressure it pulls you back to that sweet spot where your state of mind is balanced and at peace. I will admit there are times when this is easier said than done.

Seeing the worst

As I have said, managing and dealing with mistakes has challenged me at times. Consequently there have been times I've ended up playing too safe due to the fear of making a mistake. Although most of my professional practices are centred on staying in the here and now, there are a few times when I indulge my imagination. Now, when I'm feeling a little anxious about making mistakes, I deliberately play through in my mind those potential events that I'm frightened about happening out there. I imagine myself making crucial mistakes at key times and seeing the disappointment of my team-mates, fans and the coaches. In the face of this I then imagine myself looking calm, collected, peaceful and happy.

By imagining such events, they lose their impact to frighten me and damage my performance.

Maybe this is because in some shape or form we attract what we are fearful of. When I can comfortably stand toe-to-toe with my fears I'm able to show that they have no power over me. This is a tool I try to use as often as possible. One of the key times is in the dressing room before matches. Obviously it doesn't stop negative events from happening, but it's another strategy to help me react well. Over time it has helped me deal mentally with mistakes and setbacks on the pitch when they arise.

A good example of using this technique concerns Gary Megson who, after the team lost, would usually give us a piece of his mind. As I've said, his will to win is unbelievable, in some ways a mindset similar to Ronaldo's. Although at times this talking-to was intense for the players, I used it to my advantage. Before I stepped out onto the football pitch I would imagine Megson screaming and shouting. This would allow me to see the worst happening in the dressing room, feel comfortable with it, and be able to play with freedom and calmness without worrying too much about what would happen after the game if we didn't win. Nine times out of ten I work hard to stay present in the here-and-now. This is one of the few times that I indulge my imagination.

Learning how to manage such intensity was a great experience. I realised that if I can live in my mind with the worst happening then it becomes far easier to deal with if it actually happens. Being present with what I'm scared of in my mind is liberating.

Like the previous tool, playing down the importance of the performance, this tool helps me to let some steam off when the pressure starts to rise. When I feel the pressure and the expectation bounce around in the dressing room, 'seeing the worst' and feeling comfortable with various negative scenarios, is a great way to feel a little looser.

Whenever I make mistakes now I don't get that immediate adrenaline rush of panic. This technique in particular has trained my mind to expect mistakes and not lose my cool when they arrive. Exposure to the things I fear continues to help me be courageous and not play overly safe. It is a constant challenge but one I continue to rise to.

Acceptance

It is so easy to get caught up in negative thinking when things aren't going my way. My immediate response is to try and think my way out of trouble. My natural instinct whenever I feel pain is to do what I can to get rid of it; I think that's the fighter mentality within me. When I follow this path I waste energy and at times it has made me feel unusually tired and fatigued. I've also noticed that the more I try to get on top of my negative thinking the harder it becomes to escape. Of late I've found that the key to this is acceptance.

To keep my engine room firing on all cylinders, instead of being swept away by negative emotions, I try to observe them and let them go. As I've said, they are natural occurrences and surrendering to them and accepting them helps me move with these negative forces instead of battling with them. First thing in the morning and last thing at night are also nice times to let go and surrender to my current state of mind, without trying too hard to fix or change how I'm feeling.

Accepting and in some ways surrendering to any turmoil in my mind has become the quickest way for me to come out of any storms that I may be experiencing in my head. As I spoke about in Chapter 2, it's a bit like having a fire in your head. Overthinking and over-analysing is like throwing wood on the fire: it only feeds and strengthens it. The best way to let the fire burn out is to leave it alone. Accept that it is there, know that it is okay and there is nothing you need to do immediately and it will gradually lose its power and die out.

Finding silence

The times when I'm not feeling my best is when I start hearing my inner critic. This probably happens to everyone. My own inner critic has on many occasions told me I'm not playing my best, and when I start listening to that critic and questioning myself, I can end up losing confidence and depleting my reserves of energy. My inner critic at its worst will blame the circumstances I find myself in and make me feel like a victim.

But there are times when my inner critic has done some good and helped to drive me forwards. It can encourage me to improve on discipline and my work ethic. However bad this self-criticism makes me feel, it helps me to fight, compete and work hard on the football pitch. The inner critic keeps my teeth sharp.

The trick is to know when to listen to your inner critic, and when to switch it off. A way of dealing with my inner critic when it is not useful, is to turn down the volume of its comments, which in my case leaves me with a silent and clear mind.

One of the most effective times to use this is on the Sunday after a poor performance on Saturday. It is incredibly easy to get lost in negative thoughts the day after a difficult match.

Another principle to quieten the inner critic that I've worked on is learning to listen to the silence. One saying or mantra Sam and I have used to try to clear my mind and get re-grounded to the present moment is to 'listen to the silence'. This saying forces me to try and find silence in what I was doing. I continue to find that when I'm silent the right behaviour naturally follows. It is the ultimate answer to the problems I've faced at important times.

Although nine times out of ten there is noise and competing distractions around me it is still possible to find silence when necessary. If I find my mind is disturbed or lost in thought, tracking down my own silence at that point helps me to regain my composure and sense of self.

The saying 'listen to the silence' encourages me to find it, as a challenge: it provides something for me to track down. When there is noise and you start looking for and listening to the silence, you actively get your mind settling on what is going on around you. You become mindful and are pulled back to your present moment. Finding inner silence continues to help me control my emotions and get my general state nicely balanced.

Getting physical

As a rule of thumb the times I feel like my engine room is not working properly is when my focus goes inwards, away from the here and now. One of the earlier techniques that I worked on was to train my focus onto my physical senses. At every opportunity if I get focused on my physical experiences, including what I'm touching, seeing, smelling, and sometimes even tasting, I find that my emotional state naturally finds its balance. It is the sensations, felt by all the physical senses, that I need to pull my awareness back to when I'm feeling negative.

During tough matches when there is a natural break in play I will set the task of tuning into my physical senses. Sometimes I set the task of counting ten deep breaths, or fixating on one spot on the football pitch like a nearby patch of grass. This kind of focus allows everything buzzing around inside me to settle, and it allows me to recover my composure.

Final thoughts

The main indicator of my engine room working properly is when I have a balanced state of mind and I feel in control. Fortunately I've built up a collection of tools and mindsets that keep my mind calm and composed, especially during heated football matches. However, it's not always easy to keep my emotions in check in the world of football as I've found out!

Magic reminders

- The biggest predictor of whether or not I play well on the football pitch comes down to my overall emotional state.
- When I'm feeling a healthy mix of calmness and excitement I find the composure I need to play my best football.
- When my heart rate is too high I start to try too hard and end up losing control and composure.
- Using deep breathing techniques is a reliable way for me to keep my emotions well balanced on and off the football pitch.
- Imagining the things that could go wrong out on the football pitch beforehand helps my mind and my body feel comfortable with negative outcomes. It takes the pressure off and lets me play more freely without fear.

- Finding silence in my mind helps me to find my natural game and play with instinct. It turns off any negative noise in my head and it keeps my emotions in a good place.
- Emotions are contagious within a team. It is easy to allow the minds of those around you to influence your own state of mind.

FOUR

BATTLE MANAGEMENT

Making sure that I turn up and give 100% every day is where success lies for me.

Seeing my professional life as a healthy battle gives me the right intensity I need to perform at my best. Over the years I've spent a lot of time developing routines which I use both on and off the pitch. They give me quite a fixed way of going about my business which has evolved through trial and error, drawn from my earlier years of intensive training with Ronaldo all way the up to my work with Sam. It's a battle management plan that works for me.

Central to my plan is that I don't fixate on an upcoming match, but treat each day as equally important. And each day is a battle that needs to be won. Having this focus has stopped me from putting unhelpful pressure on myself before a match. This chapter provides a bird's-eye view of the platform that gears me up mentally and physically to compete every week.

Start as you mean to go on

From a young age I developed a mature way to prepare for training and matches. Ronaldo and I, even at the age of ten, conducted ourselves in a professional manner. Mentally Ronaldo and I are similar, it's just quality-wise he is a long way ahead of me. Combine his quality and his mental strength and you see why he is the greatest player in football. As I've mentioned before, we would even go a step further and uncover new and innovative ways to improve. At the age of 11 Ronaldo and I would sneak into the gym at 11.30 p.m. and work hard on our strength and speed. We would regularly go to one of Sporting Lisbon's mini-pitches late at night and do 1-vs-1s where we would put weights on our feet and improve each other: me as a defender and Ronaldo as an attacking player. We would spend an hour straight doing this. These are just a couple of the amazing extra sessions that we put ourselves through.

The energy we had when we were kids! We could play game after game every day. It's different now, where the intensity on match Saturdays is so high, you need to make sure you give your body ample time to recover and rebuild. Although I've been with Ronaldo from the beginning of his footballing journey I've never known what he does after matches, if anything. When we met up last summer, I discovered that Ronaldo has a very similar recovery session to mine. It was a reassuring coincidence that we are both instinctively doing what is right for our bodies. I think this was born from the work ethic we developed very early on in our careers.

Both of us have the professionalism which makes us take care of ourselves and respect our bodies. The way I see it, preparation is a week-long process. It is not just an hour or so before a game, it is all that I've done throughout the week added up. If I've worked hard during the week and done everything to work on my mind, body and spirit I will come to the match feeling good and able to be my best.

The funnel

Other than developing a very healthy work ethic from an early age, I've recently worked with Sam to finesse my general match preparation. Sam shared a story with me about the time he delivered a private workshop for a client who had just returned from the army. Sam explained how some military personnel have what they call a funnel approach to engaging with the enemy. For example, if they are expected to meet and engage with the enemy within a week, at the beginning of the week they are more focused on deep thinking and planning, and when they engage with the enemy it is all about action and having a programmed response. Again, as you get closer to engaging with the enemy, you do less and less thinking. You are funnelled from a place of deep thinking into a place of automatic behaviour.

My preparation to a match is very similar. At the beginning of the week, we discuss in length what needs to be focused on, based on the last performance, and how I was feeling in training. We practise the techniques and/or interventions in training and then look at some simple reminders in the actual match to make sure that they are applied automatically.

Following this vein of thought, there are other important ways in which too much thinking just before a match is counter-productive. When I'm in the dressing room, just before I step out onto the football pitch, the most effective team-talks are those that are short and sharp. When I was playing at Charlton under Phil Parkinson I noticed that he was very good at this. His talks were always about key processes that we would need to follow out on the football pitch and were always straight to the point. He didn't get us thinking too much. It was all about execution. This stopped me over-thinking and kept my mind focused on action.

The term Sam and I use is 'paralysis by analysis'. Thought is proven to hinder action. Keeping my mind external and staying glued on the physical sensations around me is critical, especially just before I'm about to perform.

In the sporting arena, over-thinking will mean I lose sharpness, my shape, and most importantly my flow. Naturally though, when you are performing on the pitch, there are natural breaks in play when you are more likely to allow your mind to wander and over-think. When the whistle blows at match-time I can operate on auto-pilot and just follow my instincts. Starting to think about what needs to be done on the football pitch makes everything slow and clumsy.

Core routines

Getting my preparation right before matches has always been important to ensure I am in the right state of mind. However, my approach to getting prepared for performances is quite flexible. I don't rely on the need to do things in a specific order; the main thing is to ensure I'm in a balanced and calm state of mind. It's not so much about what I do during my preparation but more about how I do it. As long I'm in the correct mindset I am strengthening my chances of taking this feel-good factor out onto the football pitch.

On a practical level my general preparation starts with eating a healthy breakfast in the mornings, and ends with me getting my kit ready for the match. It sounds very simple, but I am a big believer in not over-complicating something that doesn't need to be complicated. Physically I am always well prepared and since working with Sam I understand the importance of ensuring that I have a balanced state of mind before performing. The good thing about pre-match preparation and preparation during the week is that I'm in control of what I do. The same applies to routines that I use when I'm on the football pitch, despite the fact that the game is always changing.

I have more structured routines on the football pitch than I do off it. Most of my routines in this context are designed to get my mind back in check when the pressure of the game heats up. These core routines come into play when I give a foul away, when disagreements break out amongst team-mates and players, the fans start getting agitated, or you feel criticism coming from the bench. Towards the end of matches, just before half-time, and conceding goals are also critical times that I need try to find time to squeeze in one of my routines. Generally after these events there is a quick break in play that allows me to exercise my routines.

However, the most important time for one or more of my routines to come into play is just after a mistake. In the past my reaction to making a mistake would have been unpredictable. Sometimes I would drift into my own mind and mentally beat myself up, or with luck would be able to shrug it off. My response to mistakes on the football pitch is the critical factor in the overall success of my game. Wanting to make sure I moved on quickly from any mistakes I made, I worked with Sam to ensure my mind stayed in a good place.

The very first technique that we brought into my performance was imagining that Mr Bean was telling me off for making the mistake. Actually, Mr Bean is very popular in Portugal and I've always found him funny. Inviting light humour into my experience of making mistakes has helped me not to beat myself up or to take the event too seriously.

The technique of deep breathing, which I mentioned in Chapter 3, is also a great method of keeping my head clear after making a mistake and calming me down in all heated situations. Stopping to breathe deeply, and focus on that breathing, brings me back to my body and stops the thoughts and ideas in my head from distracting me.

Another routine that I use from time to time when my focus has been broken by events on the football pitch is allowing my mind to drift outside of myself and see what is going on from afar. It's a bit like watching the match I'm involved in as if it were on TV for a short period of time. It allows me to step outside of myself and get some headspace.

These routines all have the purpose of keeping me grounded and they prevent me from becoming lost in my thinking. Anything that keeps me in the here-and-now seems to work for me. It does require discipline to do this all of the time and there are still plenty of times when I forget because I've got caught up in my emotions.

Under the spotlight

Learning from the past and being able see the events of the past objectively and critically has helped me to get my overall battle management right and ultimately *win the day*. It is a routine that at times I've neglected, but whenever I do make the time I immediately see the benefits. To learn from past matches, Sam and I regularly get recordings which we sit down and analyse. We use them to talk about the positive and negative aspects of each game. This process of player analysis has taught me to see mistakes and areas of weakness in a positive light without getting bogged down with any of the negatives. It has also contributed to ensuring I *win the day*. If it's clear where I've made mistakes and we can identify obvious ways of improvement, then I can fine-tune the focus of my day-to-day training as well as special training for the upcoming matches.

From a young age your football coaches train you to do things correctly and not to make mistakes. It is only with experience that I've recognised the importance of making mistakes. After doing considerable player analysis over the years I've realised that some of my best games are when I made several mistakes but kept going with a sustained desire to make things happen. If I haven't made any mistakes in a game I probably haven't had a big presence in the game. If I've made a few mistakes it is likely that, for every mistake, I've made several positive actions and moves have followed. Mistakes are often now a part of my game that I almost hope for. If I play for 90 minutes not making a single mistake, it is probably because I wasn't particularly active in the game. Interestingly, whenever I've won man-of-the-match its been in a game where I've made mistakes.

Player analysis has certainly helped me to feel comfortable with making mistakes. Seeing them on a screen helps me to step out of myself, be objective, and see mistakes as inevitable. Getting caught up in worrying about the mistakes of a previous game is a thing of the past.

Checking in

I demonstrated in Chapter 2 how important it is for me to control my emotions from day to day. One of my core routines is to check in regularly during the day with my feelings to see where my emotional state is. Being conscious about how I am feeling gives me the awareness to do something about it. When I fail to check in, it's possible for me to get lost in my emotions, which has resulted in me losing my control and discipline. If I am aware of tension building up I can address the causes before I get into trouble.

Some of the key times for me to check my emotional state include travelling to training, during training, the night before matches, warming up before matches, in the dressing room before matches, during breaks in play, and just after games. By being aware of my mood I am able to adjust it accordingly and stay nicely balanced. Checking in to your feelings is a mindfulness practice and there is more on this in Chapter 5.

Winding down

A core routine which I use without fail after a performance is making time to wind down. Time to myself after working hard is really important as it keeps my motivation levels high. I love being with the family and making sure that we all eat together. Picking the kids up from school and taking them swimming are two regular activities that help me to switch off from work, concentrate on something else that really matters to me, and unwind.

Back in the days when we were at Sporting Lisbon, Ronaldo and I would regularly go to the local shopping centre and hang out with some of our other friends: just to switch off from football, for a while. The more football dominates my life, the more likely I am to feel the inevitable pressure. When football is everything you have, and things don't go your way on the pitch, life starts to look very dark. This is why I develop interests off the pitch so that I know football is only one component of my life.

Outside of the football arena I have a variety of interests that keep me grounded. Football is such a dominant part of my life that I have to be disciplined in making time for other things, or it can overrun my life. Being a family man, much of my enjoyment stems from the time I spend with my wife and children. My kids are always full of life and just being around them brings me peace and happiness. I love taking them swimming and to the local parks. Seeing them run around fills me with energy and inspiration. My kids definitely take me outside of myself and remind me that there is so much more to life than what happens on the football pitch.

The physical demands that are placed on me by football also remind me that downtime is crucial. I often visit some of the local health spas to unwind and relax, especially during the winter months, to give the mind and body time to recuperate.

Most nights before I fall asleep I try to make time to read. Because my first language is Portuguese, reading English books requires more attention. I see this as an advantage because it keeps my mind focused on the pages in front of me as opposed to wandering back to football. Mostly I read non-fiction books because I have a hunger to learn new things. Several of my favourite books are about self-help and human psychology. Two of these which I keep beside me are *Thinking Body, Dancing Mind* by Chungliang Al Huang and Jerry Lynch (1994) and Paul McKenna's *Change Your Life In Seven Days* (2005). Both have had a positive impact on the way I view life and have reinforced my desire to stay happy.

Pushing outside the comfort zone

Being mindful of the role that comfort zones play in my life has given me a keener eye on how to manage my performances and how I train. The comfort zone is the space that I want to stay in when I'm either feeling anxious, demotivated or want to play it extra safe. The choice of staying in the comfort zone or stepping out of it is often the difference between a good game and a bad one. There have been games in my career where comfort zones have held me back and prevented me from going for it.

I believe battles are won rather than lost on the football field by being prepared to step outside the comfort zone. During those 90 minutes I need to be ready to take risks when appropriate, to put myself on the line and challenge myself. If I am not prepared to do this then my battle management has failed and I haven't turned up to the game.

Naturally when I am being courageous and pushing outside my comfort zone I make mistakes. However, the more courageous I become over time, the easier these daring actions are to complete and mistakes become less frequent.

Sometimes inaction can be more dangerous than taking action. Athletes who continue to go for it, despite making hundreds of mistakes along the way, are the ones who get to the top of their game.

As a strategy to break through my comfort zone in all areas of life, I try to set daily challenges for myself. One of these is trying to do things that I wouldn't usually do. One of the tasks Sam suggested to me was to try to touch the opposition's box as many times as possible, when it was appropriate to do so. Just by being in the right place at the right time we felt I would find greater opportunities to develop my offensive game. As a result of doing this I was in the right place at the right time to score my last goal for Sheffield Wednesday which came against Wycombe Wanderers. I got myself in a position to back-up our forward players and found myself on the edge of the box on the right-hand side of the football pitch. The ball hit the post and rebounded straight to my feet, which I was able instinctively to hit with my right foot and guide into the back of the net. This wouldn't have happened if I hadn't set myself the comfort-zone challenge of putting myself in new areas of the football pitch.

Sometimes when I am in the sweet spot and my football is flowing, I surprise my mind and my body by being daring in ways I didn't even plan; it feels like I take courageous action effortlessly without any thinking. When I allow myself to stop thinking about what I need to do in order to push outside the comfort zone and find inner stillness and quiet, I take daring actions without thinking about them. They almost emerge by themselves. You just know you can do it and let instinct and training take over.

One such time was when Sheffield Wednesday played Sheffield United in League One under Dave Jones. It was a critical game if we were to get automatic promotion to the Championship. Reda Johnson took the throw-in and could see me in the prime position to make something happen. I knew if I could beat the player who was closest to me I would be able to switch the play and create an opportunity for the team to score. I got the ball, and turned my man and switched the play to Lewis Buxton. He made a quick pass to Antonio who consequently set up Chris O'Grady to score the winner. It is the most beautiful memory of my entire career in football. It was the biggest derby I've ever played in and when we scored the winning goal I went down on my knees and thanked God. Thinking back, the moment I got the ball and created an opportunity to score, it feels like I had no control over what I did. It happened so quickly and so instinctively, it as if it was written in the stars. It was an extraordinary experience that I can only put down to an intervention of faith.

The result of my actions is not what's important, it's more about having the intention and taking a step into an unknown space. Taking the safe option is usually the easier path, but the magic happens only when we do venture away from the easier road and take a risk. Again this does not mean I forget about my defensive duties but always look to ways to push and challenge myself.

One mindset that encourages me to approach every challenge on and off the football pitch with a daring and courageous mindset is the fear of having regrets. I know that I am not the most gifted footballer; that doesn't bother me. What bothers me is looking in the mirror knowing that there was so much more I could have done to be successful.

I am determined to do everything within my power in life to be happy and successful. Not wanting to live with any regrets forces me to squeeze everything out of each day and know that I didn't waste it. Again this mindset was born from working with Ronaldo and going the extra mile to improve at every opportunity.

Win the day

In my world winning is a day-to-day pursuit and not only reserved for football matches. The concept of winning the day is now so central to my psychology that it's the title of my book. It is the doorway into my whole approach to life. My mantra *win the day* reminds me that as long as my focus is on taking healthy actions and doing the things within my control, when Saturday comes the match performance will take care of itself. My actions on the football pitch are nearly always a by-product of where my focus has been during the week, which is why this mindset is so important.

Developing a focus on the day-to-day, and not looking too far ahead, helps me regularly to push outside my comfort zone. Spending a little extra time on the treadmill, putting more care and attention into my choice of food, and giving my prayer time the attention it deserves are ways of making each day an extraordinary one.

Thinking about all that you want to achieve in sport and in life is great. Setting goals and having ambitions can help to keep you hungry. But it's very easy to get lost in dreams and over-imagine all of the goals you want to achieve. Focusing on such goals adds unwanted pressure to my game and makes me try too hard, get tense and become frustrated when performances are not going to plan.

One of the first steps to letting go of my goals and ambitions was to break them down into actions and processes that were in my control. How do I win football matches? What makes a good tackle? What actions would I need to take? Things like being on my toes, keeping my head up, keeping my eye on the ball and feeling light come to mind. If my mind stays focused on such actions I know that the desired outcome of making a strong tackle and hopefully winning the football match will follow. This process made me realise that by keeping my focus on actions that were in my control, the outcomes that I ultimately wanted to achieve would be a welcome by-product. Developing this action-led mindset certainly contributed to me playing every game for Sheffield Wednesday when we won promotion to the Championship Division.

So what is an action or a process? It's something that can be done right now and is within my direct control. Winning football matches, scoring goals, keeping a clean sheet, training well, and winning promotion: these are not actions but outcomes. Thinking about these different outcomes doesn't move me any closer to them. What's useful is looking at the actions I can take to increase my chances of achieving them.

There are times when I've forgotten to focus on the processes, and nearly every time it's happened my performance levels drop. I feel a little more anxious, I can fatigue quicker, and also I start trying too hard. Building a competitive mentality comes from a desire to win every moment of every day, not just in training or on the football pitch. This is what I've learned over the years especially growing up with Ronaldo. My 'winning the day' mentality has put me in good stead to get as much as I can from life.

Process success

When I met him, Sam Kotadia had already been working with Phil Parkinson at Colchester United. Later I heard about some of Parky's early experiences working with Sam. They managed to install an action-led mindset within Colchester during their historic promotion to the Championship Division. Parky and Sam would talk with the team and identify what actions they needed to take in order to win football matches. All of the actions that the team came up with would then be printed on posters and displayed all around the dressing room to ensure everyone stayed glued to what they needed to do in order to play well. The coaches would also never talk about winning games and beating the opposition, instead their communication was focused on actions: being first to the ball, watching your runner, staying on your toes, and getting a picture of some of the coach's action-led language. After bringing this in during the 2005/2006 season the club went on a 12-match unbeaten streak in the league and found themselves going on to play Chelsea in the fifth round of the F.A. Cup that year.

Staying focused on taking the right day-to-day actions makes the week a productive one. The month becomes successful and the season becomes positive. The accolades I've won, including Player of the Year at Charlton Athletic, Player of the Year at Sheffield Wednesday and runner-up Player of the Year, show what can result from putting this principle into action.

Loving my craft and not being pre-occupied with winning and losing is important to me. There are times, however, that I think it is impossible in professional sport to get your mind away from the winning and losing. Fans don't want to see their team lose, irrespective of how much the team were process-focused during the game. Again, however strange it may sound, not thinking about winning has helped me to win.

Leaving no stone unturned

My hunger to win the day and explore every avenue of self-improvement was born from working alongside Ronaldo. Both of us encouraged each other to hunt for excellence and go the extra mile in making ourselves more successful on the football pitch. We spent time perfecting our routines and challenging one another every day. One of our favourite drills was 1-vs-1s, where Ronaldo would put weights on his legs and practise trying to beat me with his step-overs. We also used to watch the runners at Sporting Lisbon who had a running circuit around the stadium and we used to go and talk with them. The idea of studying the runners was not mine, it was all due to Ronaldo's obsession with perfection. One of the runners we spoke to was the Portuguese sprinter Francis Obikwelu. We wanted to learn how to be quicker so we would often ask for his advice on correct running technique.

This is just one of many examples of how we tried our best to be even better than the other players. What is remarkable about Ronaldo is that he didn't need to go to extra lengths to be even better, he was already the best and likely to become a world-class player even without the desire to want to keep improving. But he would leave no stone unturned in his search for betterment. Complacency is something totally foreign to us both.

Final thoughts

Never looking too far ahead has been critical to anything that I've achieved in football. Treating every day the same has trained me not only to work hard in the big moments but in every moment. I've found over the years that when I'm in the habit of doing this I naturally find the right mindset for big games and am able to recover from the occasional setback.

Magic reminders

- My early years in football with Ronaldo helped me to develop the discipline to work hard every day and be the best I can be.
- Over the years I've learned to focus on the actions I need to take, as opposed to focusing on the outcomes I'm aiming for. By being action focused I've found I am much more likely to be successful on and off the football pitch.
- Watching past games has helped me to see my performances clearly. I am then able to take what I've learned constructively into the next game.
- Positive results always follow when I push outside of my comfort zone.
- I treat every day the same. No day is more important than any other. This has got me to focus on being the best I can be each day irrespective of what I am doing. As long as I am focused on winning each day I naturally turn up on Saturdays with the right mindset.
- Constantly learning and looking for new ways to improve will always be in my mind. This will ensure that success is a journey and not a destination.

FIVE

THE MAGIC OF MINDFULNESS

Being attentive to the present moment is where I my find success.

For me mindfulness is about cherishing the moment and truly paying attention to it. It's about making every day of life worth living and not taking anything for granted. More traditional definitions talk about learning to acknowledge your feelings, thoughts and bodily sensations calmly and without judgement.

Other definitions of mindfulness are: being aware of your awareness, paying attention to moment-to-moment experiences with heartfulness, and 'just being, not doing'.

Feeling mindful

My thoughts, whether positive or negative, have often blinded me to what is going on in the here and now. In the world of football my mind often drifts: into the future, imagining how my upcoming games will go, and also into the past, stewing over poor performances. Consequently I've then become mindless to what is happening around me and not able to give the present moment the attention it deserves.

For many years I saw sports psychology as a way to fix these problems in focusing. But although the suggestions and techniques did help to bring some control, I was still looking outside of myself for the answer. Mindfulness training has brought me a relief from this constant searching for quick fixes, and has been the most important component of my mental training over the past five years. Just *being* and having a clear awareness of the present moment has become a critical part of getting ready to perform and being able to enter the arena feeling resourceful. Mindfulness has opened up the reality that mental training and mental conditioning for all performances is a moment-to-moment pursuit. It is not something that you do by turning up at an office and going through a structured programme. It is a way of life and not just reserved for the football pitch.

At times it's possible for me to be absorbed totally in the present moment, without looking forwards or backwards, and it's then that my personal power is strong. Being fully focused in my actions, I can become lost in my performance in a healthy way. This state is amazing: you lose all sense of time. Everything feels effortless and natural. Time flies; 90 minutes feel like five. The most appropriate word to describe this state is peace. You feel in harmony with your environment. It's not just a phenomenon that is reserved for the football pitch, it's something I experience in other areas of my life when I'm feeling particularly connected. For example the time I spend with Ronaldo is a great example of mindfulness in action. When I'm in Ronaldo's presence I really feel connected to the present moment. Everything around me becomes a blur and I feel completely engaged in what he is saying. There have been times when we have been so deeply engaged in the present moment that we laugh uncontrollably, even in a restaurant with everybody looking at us! We have a deep happiness when we are together, and when others see us laugh together they start laughing too. I believe we all have a deep desire to be lost in the present moment which is why

I think such experiences can be so infectious. This is how I know that I'm in the present moment. I lose my sense of self and all of my focus is completely on him. We are engrossed in one another, often reminiscing, to the point that we lose all sense of time. We forget everything and we live in that moment together.

I have this experience too in my sessions with Sam and in the presence of close friends and family. An intensive four-hour session has felt more like 30 minutes long. Again we get so engrossed in what we are talking about that time disappears. Whenever I'm truly present, whether on the football pitch or in the company of my close friends, time seems to melt away.

Practising mindfulness is incredibly important on the football pitch. When you are on centre stage with thousands of football fans watching you, remaining present is incredibly challenging. The social pressures of team-mates, coaches and fans often lead me to over-thinking and retreating within myself. Mindfulness practices have in some ways raised the bar and stopped me from getting lost in emotions and thoughts.

So what is it like being mindful? Try pretending that you are watching your life on a wide-screen TV with you taking the position of the commentator. By commenting on what you are doing you become more aware of your actions and consequently you put more care and attention into them. When I do this I also find that I've a greater awareness of what is happening and make better decisions without too much thought and pre-planning. You can also observe your thoughts and emotions as an outsider, and let them go. The hardest thing about mindfulness is keeping up practising it. Constantly being present and aware of your feelings and sensations without judgement requires hard work.

F.A. Cup mindfulness

A memorable experience of being totally absorbed in the present moment was a game I played against Tottenham in the F.A. Cup. The game was played at White Hart Lane; it was an occasion the whole team were very much looking forward to. To this day I remember the game vividly: the smell of the grass, the sights and sounds of everything around me. Time stood still as I was so absorbed in everything that I was feeling and sensing. Although the team lost, individually I had an excellent game. Being totally present and mindful was the reason behind this success.

The way this affected me was that I felt all of my actions were more precise and I had a better read of the game. In some ways the game played itself. This may sound strange, but it felt effortless and just flowed. Mindfulness has encouraged me to let go, to embrace and accept my present experiences without judgement. When I find stillness and peace I realise everything I'm looking for is inside of me.

When I'm in the groove of regular mindfulness practice, I start putting less emphasis on the big games because they just become other moments in my flow. Every day and every new moment are treated the same. This helps me to find freedom, peace of mind and the ability to shape the course of the game when I perform. Again, because I'm naturally a little anxious and over-driven, this sense of peace and flow from mindfulness allows me to be natural.

An important shift for me was seeing the connection between my day-to-day actions and how they influence my performance. I used to believe improving my performance on the football pitch happened during training and during matches. However, my longest stretches of consistent performance have come from building a disciplined mindset off the pitch. This then naturally flowed effortlessly into my game. It is easier said than done, for sure, but this means putting fully focused care and attention into every daily action, whether it's brushing my teeth, doing the washing-up or preparing a meal. Every moment is an opportunity to build a winning and successful mentality. Being present and mindful of my daily actions in my private life makes me find it naturally easier to play well come Saturday.

Returning home

Mindfulness helps me not to be judgemental about my experiences. When I do something wrong which causes me anxiety or pain, I need to return home to a calm state as soon as possible. In the past, my immediate reaction to pain was to try and fight it. Mindfulness helps me to respect pain by observing it, sitting alongside it, and recognising that it is an unavoidable part of life. Pain comes and it goes. Once you start feeding the pain with negative thinking and negative judgement, it just becomes stronger and lasts longer. In Chapter 2 I talked about how fear also behaves like a fire, which will die out if not fed with more fuel. Pain is similar: the moment I experience pain there's a rush of panic and fear. As long as I don't feed the mind with negative thoughts about what has just happened, my mind naturally returns to a peaceful and clear state. When I'm able to accept pain and move with it, my mind and body return to a calm state.

This is what happens on the football pitch. If my play has cost the team a goal and there's a rush of panic. Instead of learning to accept and be mindful of the pain, my instinct is to get rid of that feeling as quickly as possible. If I then start over-thinking about the setback and what I need to do to stop the same error happening again, I become tight, lose my flow and the wheels come off. But if I allow the pain and panic to sit with me without judgeing them, I maintain my flow and my composure; the pain then subsides by itself.

It's not feeling negative that stops me playing my best football, it's whether I start paying the negative too much attention. Strange but true: if and when I have negative thoughts my flow is not disturbed so long as I can be non-judgemental. Thoughts come and go, so I observe them, and let them move on and eventually out of focus. The art of allowing this to happen is what the guy said after walking across a bed of hot coals: 'the trick is not minding that it hurts'. If I can sit with the pain without battling what has just happened with my thoughts, I return to a natural state of calm, and for me my best football naturally follows.

Watching traffic

So how do you deal with negative thoughts, and not let them rule your emotions? There's a helpful image in a book called *Headspace* which explained it this way … Imagine that you are sitting by the side of a busy road and cars are streaming by you. Some of these cars are desirable: flashy new sports cars, whilst others are old and run down. Imagine that the flashy sports cars are your positive thoughts and emotions, whilst the less desirable cars are the negative thoughts and emotions. Naturally we want to jump on the positive thoughts and keep them in our sight as long as possible, whereas when we experience the negative, we want to get rid of it as quickly as possible.

Mindfulness has taught me to value every experience that flows in and out of my focus without trying to fix, keep or manipulate what comes and goes. This doesn't mean I stop enjoying the highs or feeling the lows, but that I keep a sense of flow. This flow is critical to success in all walks of life. Again, it's not about the nature of your thoughts, it's about what you do with them. Continually I find that I can keep my composure and my A-game even when there may be a constant flow of negative thoughts. Positive changes can only take place in the present moment. The less attention I have on what I'm doing right now, the weaker the action becomes.

My breakthrough came one day during training. It was the strangest experience but it changed my thinking about sport and life in general. All those regular negative thoughts and emotions about my game became separate from me. No longer was I caught up in them, I let the thoughts be, and naturally they moved on and I returned to a more peaceful and grounded state of mind. Consequently I was able to play good football despite where my mind was.

As I've said, negative thoughts and emotions don't necessarily lead to a poor performance: what does create a poor action is getting stuck in negative thinking, which disrupts the flow. The same applies to positive thoughts and emotions. If I get too attached to good experiences, when the tide turns and there's a setback, it leaves me surprised, angry and frustrated. I can feel helpless to recover the situation. So, when I'm lucky enough to have rewarding experiences, I acknowledge, observe and respect them, knowing they will not last. Just as when there are negative experiences I also observe them, respect them, and know they too cannot last.

Aikido

An image that helps me deal with negative thinking compares getting lost in negative thinking with being in a storm, or receiving a blow from a fighter. This encourages me to blend with the strike of the fighter, surrender to the storm, in order to come of out of my negative thinking quicker.

In the martial art of Aikido, the defending fighter moves *with* the motion of his attacker, as opposed to *against* it. The defender diffuses the power of the hit so the attacking force loses its power to cause damage. The same thing applies when a negative event happens. Although it is still there, by responding in such a way that you accept and move with it, it loses its power to cause you real harm. Tackling it head-on makes the negative force even more destructive.

Letting go

Another metaphor of mindfulness introduced to me a few years ago is the *sand mandala*. There is an ancient Buddhist tradition which involves the creation of intricate patterns, called mandalas, sometimes using sand. Immediately after creating them, Buddhists would destroy the mandala to illustrate the importance of not getting attached to your creations, or anything else for that matter. The same applies to great performances: once they are over, let them go and focus on creating the next great one.

Anchored on the present moment

When the mind wanders, it is the dedication and the commitment to keep pulling it back to the present moment that matters. If you build this, you develop real inner strength and power. It is easy to get stuck in both positive and negative emotions, which take our focus away and put us on autopilot. Mindfulness is about being non-judgemental of what comes in and out of your waking focus. It is about being authentically awake to the here and now. Although you want your automatic actions and processes to make your performances flow effortlessly, it doesn't mean that you shouldn't be present and aware of your performance.

More time

One of the benefits I've found of working on mindfulness is that you create more time for yourself. Everything becomes clearer and you start seeing things as they really are. Being out on the football pitch is a prime example of how, when you are mindful, it feels like you create more time for yourself. I guess because you are not putting energy into wasteful thinking, you are able to put all your focus and energy into the present moment. You have a deeper connection with what is going on around you, you are able to react and respond in a sharper and more controlled manner because you are not wasting time getting lost in your thoughts.

If my head is busy with thoughts during a football match, when I receive the ball I often think I've less time than I actually have in deciding what I should do with it. Consequently I would snatch at the pass I was trying to execute, or generally make a poor decision. When I'm mindful and focused on the present moment, I'm more composed and relaxed, so I can get a picture of the situation, take a controlled touch of the ball and make a good decision on how to proceed.

There was one game that stood out for me when I started to become more conscious of the extra time I had on the ball. It was against Yeovil last season when I developed a mantra to remind me of this. I said in my mind 'when I get the ball and I have touch, I know I will have time'. Consequently I developed the freedom and swagger to hold the ball and be more commanding in the midfield and not want to off-load it quicker than I needed to.

The power of prayer

Mindfulness may have emerged from the practices of Buddhism, but its principles are being used today by people of many other faiths and of none. As a Catholic, I have a deep relationship with God and the power of prayer is important in my life. Prayer has always been a doorway to calmness and peace throughout my life. When I prayed to God for someone to help with my psychology, I was introduced to Sam, and this for me is confirmation of the power of my faith. Faith can bring the right people into your life at the right time.

From a very early age I grew up praying with my dad. When I was very young I never quite understood what my dad was doing but felt compelled to be with him when he was praying. It was my father who opened me up to this important and sacred practice in my life. Funnily enough it was only very recently that my son decided to sit with me, in a very similar to way to how I sat with my dad, and start praying. He felt drawn to what I was doing in exactly the same way I was drawn to my father. When I pray I surrender and let go of my thinking to God. Primarily I ask that he looks after my family and keeps us healthy. I also reflect on what I'm grateful for and ask for strength in testing times. I'm totally absorbed in what I'm doing; it is very difficult to distract me when I'm locked in prayer. I remember when Ronaldo saw me praying as a kid he was very intrigued. He asked me what I was doing, but at the time I couldn't speak with him because I was so immersed in the process.

In my house in Sheffield there is a room I use only for prayer and that helps me to get into the right mindset. The danger of following the same routine every day is that it's so easy to go on auto-pilot and not be totally present. I make sure that this never happens when I pray, so that I feel connected with God when I share my thoughts.

The very act of making the time to sit quietly in this sacred way helps me to be present and mindful throughout the day.

Since working with Sam I've found that I can enter this sacred space in all areas of my daily life. It doesn't just have to be reserved for the room in which I pray. I've learned that this deeper connection with God and the present moment can be practised during everyday events.

Training for mindfulness

The spaces between events are the times I most regularly find the opportunity to practise mindfulness: waiting to pick up the kids from school, speaking to people, getting ready to go to training and even when you are eating, are all times when you can train your mind. If you put your heart and soul into being the best you can be in every moment, irrespective of how unimportant the occasion, when the big events arrive you naturally have the right focus. Here are my top mindfulness training activities that I've made a way of life.

Eating and drinking

Whenever I'm preparing a meal, I focus on the sensations I have from the sight, textures and smell of the food. I ask myself what the food looks like and how it smells. How does it feel on my hands? What can I hear as it cooks? When you ask yourself these questions, it forces you to observe and take note of what is around you and ground yourself to your bodily sensations away from your thoughts.

As I eat, I deliberately count the amount of times that I chew to draw attention to the process. And during my meal

I'm also conscious of the nutrition that the food is giving me, and feel thankful for it.

Driving routines

While driving, I actively comment in my head on the things that I'm observing. This helps me to be active with what I'm seeing and hearing, as opposed to being passive. In other words, I've a voice inside my head that describes what is going on around me. It also focuses my attention on the here and now. One of the precepts of mindfulness is to do one thing at a time, so I avoid eating, talking or listening to music while driving, and just concentrate on driving.

My body scan

One of my many mindfulness routines is to systematically scan my body for any sensations I can detect. I start by placing my focus on my toes and slowly concentrating on each section of my body all the way up to my head. It can take one to two minutes to do this. I notice how each and every part of my body feels, without judgement. If a particular part of my body feels tight or uncomfortable, I observe it. I don't try to change it. The exercise really helps me to tune into my body before a performance. My body is my tool so it is important that I know it intimately.

Staying selfless

When I step onto the pitch I take five minutes to soak up all of the information I receive from my senses. I ground myself by noticing the smell of the grass, the feeling of my feet on the ground, the sounds of the fans, and freshness of the air. This helps me to be completely immersed in my physical senses and the present moment.

Sometimes on the pitch there is a break in play. To stop my focus from going inwards I pull my attention to my team-mates and observe their positions and how they appear to be feeling. As a defensive midfielder I'm always conscious of where I am in relation to my team-mates and the opposition. I like feeling connected with everyone around me, it makes me aware of my responsibilities in a positive way.

Breathing routines

Whenever I've a quiet moment in the dressing room, on the coach, or in a hotel room, I count my breathing. I count with each breath in and every breath out. This allows me to practise mindfulness and focus on the process of breathing, noticing the sensation of the breath as I count. Often I will just pick a random figure and count to that number. The counting process helps me to trust my footballing ability and not over-analyse what I need to do.

Communicating with others

On match days, whether I'm on the pitch or on the bench, I try to be mindful of how I communicate with each person. I encourage myself to feel love and compassion when I'm listening and speaking to them. It's not always easy to do this, especially when I've expected to be in the starting eleven and end up on the bench. Footballers naturally want to play every game they can, and when this is not possible it's hard to stay positive. I'm proud to know that I'm unconditionally supportive of my team-mates, irrespective of whether or not I'm playing on the Saturday.

Eastern ways

'Only as a [spiritual] warrior can one withstand the path of knowledge. A warrior cannot complain or regret anything. His life is an endless challenge and challenges cannot possibly be good or bad. Challenges are simply challenges. The basic difference between an ordinary man and a warrior is that a warrior takes everything as a challenge, while an ordinary man takes everything as a blessing or a curse.' So says Don Juan, as quoted by Jack Kornfield in *A Path With Heart*.

Once I started to learn about mindfulness I became interested in Eastern philosophies and their overall approach of living. I learned that mindfulness goes deep into many Eastern traditions. One of the books which has had a lasting impression is by the Chicago Bulls coach Jerry Lynch, called *Thinking Body Dancing Mind*. It describes Eastern psychology, which I feel drawn to. Among the principles of acceptance, learning to come to terms with fear, finding flow, and being true to yourself, the book paints a very interesting picture of the warrior spirit. It made me realise that the way of the warrior is very close to my own personal set of values when I'm at my best.

Studying the ways of the warrior, and in particular the Japanese warrior described in *The Samurai*, I learned that the true warrior spirit is not about conquering enemies or military achievement but about cultivating a way of life. The warrior mentality in the context of the footballer is about fighting to be your best not only on the pitch but also off the pitch. It is very similar to my mantra of winning the day and battling to get the most from every moment.

The film *The Last Samurai*, starring Tom Cruise, is one of my favourites as a portrayal of the warrior spirit. The

Samurai show that everything they do from day to day, from the mundane to the extraordinary, is given their undivided care and attention. Whether they are in battle, or preparing food, all of their pursuits are treated with love and respect.

The Pursuit of Happyness is another film that inspires me to follow the warrior spirit and never give in. The story of a man who is trying to juggle the responsibility of being a single parent and also build a career for himself reminds me that whatever challenges I'm faced with I must focus on winning the day and nothing else.

My introduction to mindfulness has made me realise that being focused on the present moment, without looking too far ahead, is integral to my training and how I aim to approach life. Being attentive to the present moment makes me feel at peace and in control. By adopting this mindset, I've naturally built the focus I need to perform well during the 90 minutes on the football pitch. I don't need to raise my game or the intensity of my focus because every moment is equally important.

The way of the warrior

When I think about my combative style of football and my drive to fight and leave no stone unturned to be the best I can be for myself and my team, I can see the characteristics of the ancient warrior shining through me. Over the years I've learned that if I become trapped by my thoughts I always end up being a slave to them. The warrior, on the other hand, is free from all that. I try to keep the values of the warrior close to mind. In some ways they are a blueprint to guide me to stay mindful and connected to what I hold to be true. What follows are the main truths that I try to abide by day to day to keep my warrior spirit flowing through me.

Don't move away from pain: embrace and accept it

Although none of us want to experience pain, it is unfortunately an inevitable part of life. What is not inevitable is suffering. Suffering is the negative response to pain. Pain will always be there, so learn to embrace it and respect it. You will maintain your flow. If a negative event is put upon you, then learn to make it work for you. In this sense you are able to turn straw into gold. You acknowledge pain but you do not indulge in it.

Being of service

Look to support those around you. Inspire your peers and your community to be the best they can be. Share your knowledge and your spirit to help others grow.

If you are on the centre stage you have a privileged position to be a positive influence, so I always make time for the fans and regularly visit the local hospital to show my support. Communities are so important and for me and that's why football is so special: football pulls people together.

Be true to your personal values in life

Know what's important to you in life and be sure to give it your main focus. This is critical to ensuring that you feel fulfilled and that you maintain your integrity at all times. Know what you stand for, and stand up for it.

Seek honour and responsibility

Whatever happens, always keep your honour. When things don't go your way on or off the football pitch, or in any other part of life, stand up and take responsibility. Don't look for others to blame; make sure that you are accountable for your own actions and your conduct at all times. Don't make excuses.

Show compassion whenever possible
Show compassion and forgiveness where possible. Understanding and being of service to others will nourish your mind and spirit.

Feeling fear
When you are scared, don't move away from the fear. Know that fear has a natural place in life and know that courage comes from being present with fear and not from being without it.

The powerful present
Whenever the mind wanders to the past or drifts into the future, you lose your power to be your best in the present moment. Keep your mind on the here and now, and you find true inner power.

Self-sacrifice
Know when to sacrifice yourself for the greater good. Be prepared to put yourself on the line for your team, your family and your community. Know there are no short-cuts. To rise to the challenge you need to be the best you can be every moment. Daily discipline is critical to success.

Humility
Be humble during great successes and great failures. Never start expecting anything, and never think that you are owed anything. Be patient at all times. True confidence and peace of mind is created from within. Getting your self-confidence from outside yourself has no integrity. By this I mean, if you are reliant on winning football matches and receiving praise from others in order to feel confident, you will always be looking for it. Receiving a confidence boost outside of yourself is only a fleeting positive experience, it never lasts.

Be proactive

Challenge yourself every day. Seek out experiences and tasks that test you and frighten you. Know in yourself that you are dedicated to the process of growth and make daring decisions.

Final thoughts

The practice of mindfulness has helped me make the most of every moment, and I try to collect as many ideas and metaphors to remind me how important this is. Sam shared an old poem with me that struck a chord; it's called *The Human Guest House*. It compares the human mind to owners of a guest house whose job is to welcome everyone that turns up. Whether they are unexpected, happy, or sad, treat all of your guests with honour. Like your thoughts, your guests should be welcomed without judgement and with an open mind. Just like any busy guest house, there are always new arrivals, just as there are also new thoughts and experiences to welcome into your mind. And then send them on their way.

The Human Guest House

> This being human is a guest house.
> Every morning a new arrival.
> A joy, a depression, a meanness,
> some momentary awareness comes
> as an unexpected visitor.
> Welcome and entertain them all!
> Even if they're a crowd of sorrows,
> who violently sweep your house
> empty of its furniture,
> still treat each guest honorably.
> He may be clearing you out
> for some new delight.
> The dark thought, the shame, the malice,

meet them at the door laughing,
and invite them in.
Be grateful for whoever comes,
because each has been sent
as a guide from beyond.

Jelaluddin Rumi, 13th Century Persian poet

Magic reminders

- Paying attention to my moment-to-moment experiences without judgement summarises mindfulness in action.
- Mindfulness training has brought me relief from this constant searching for quick fixes and allowed me to just be.
- When I'm in the groove of regular mindfulness practice, I start putting less emphasis on the big games because they just become other moments in the flow.
- In Eastern philosophy the notion of the warrior is similar to values by which I like to live my life, on and off the football pitch. Showing compassion, learning to sacrifice myself for the greater good, being faithful to my personal values, being humble in the face of victories, and always adopting a proactive approach to life are core principles within my warrior mentality.

SIX

STAYING ON TRACK

I never rise to the level of my expectations, I rise to the level of my training. This is why I must train well physically, mentally, emotionally and spiritually at all times.

Most of the time I know what I should be doing to ensure that my mind, body and spirit are in the right place. But having the discipline to do everything I need to do each day is another challenge. This chapter looks at the ways in which I've learned to join up the dots and make sure I stay on track each day. Reinforcing my will-power needs a range of additional methods and considerations that continue to help me make skilful decisions and keep my mind in check. This chapter addresses this.

A test of discipline

When I started to receive advice from Sam at Charlton Athletic about ways to improve my game, I thought it would be easy to put into practice. Over the years I've now realised that the real battle is not working out what I need to do in order to get better, but learning how to act on this knowledge day in, day out.

The mind requires the same training and discipline as the body. Forming new and healthy mental habits was far harder than I had ever expected, especially when things weren't going my way. Some of the growth moments in football have been when I've felt low but still managed to do what was necessary. That's where the work ethic kicks in. When I'm not playing well, it's extra hard to discipline myself to do what I should be doing. Often, when I'm feeling low, I can wallow in my sorrows and almost start indulging in them, maybe because it is the easiest thing to do at the time. I know when I'm feeling down that I should be making an effort to act in my best interests but taking the easy route is so much more appealing. Often the thought of doing something in my higher interest when I'm feeling down feels like hitting a brick wall. Taking the easy route is so much more appealing when I'm not at my best. For example, there have been several times when I skipped some of my mental and physical routines or cut them short because my emotions took control. However, being able to break through those moments is when I feel like I've grown as a person and broken negative cycles.

Once, before one of the final games of the season for Charlton, I was feeling low. It was the evening before and I did not expect to be selected for the starting eleven. I had a choice: to take the easy route and wallow in the fears of not being picked or to do something positive and take action. In this instance I made a conscious effort and watched a DVD with my family. It sounds quite basic but if I'm feeling low I often dwell on negative thinking. On this occasion I broke the negative habit.

To my surprise I was included in the final game of the season. Not only did I complete my defensive duties with flying colours I also managed to get on the score sheet and, as most of the fans know, scoring is a rare occurrence for me. In the conclusion of that season I was named Player of the Year by the fans and my team-mates. I believe that this swift change in fortune came from the moment of breaking through my negative thinking at the time and doing something positive. It moved me into a positive state of mind that I believe was the reason I was able to play well and score on the final day of the season.

As a rule when I experience extreme emotions I'm more likely to lose discipline and indulge in being negative and not give my training routines the full attention they deserve. In this example it was the deep feelings of despondency that were trying to get in the way. It's not only extreme negative feelings that get in the way but also the highs that can throw me off track. When everything is going my way on the football pitch, complacency at times can creep in. My mind starts seeing the next three points in the bag, long before Saturday has arrived.

It's another reason why being aware and mindful of your ever-shifting emotions is so critical. If I'm able to do this I gain more control over my actions and find it easier to stay on track.

Assessing the battlefield

When we were promoted to the Championship with Sheffield Wednesday, I was presuming that it would be business as usual. I had been given the accolade of Player of the Year and things were going very well. But I underestimated what would be required in order to thrive at this level. League One football is certainly more forgiving. Sam encouraged me to strengthen the level of my mental discipline by spending more time on each practice in preparation for Championship football. On reflection I should have taken his advice more to heart.

I now know the importance of getting to grips with the new working environments I find myself in. Whether it is a new league, or a new club, understanding the space that I'm working in is critical to being able to thrive and be successful. A mistake Sam believes managers regularly make when they move to a bigger club is that they assume the methods that worked at their old club will automatically transfer to their new operation. Before imposing any particular regimes on a club, he argued that you need to understand where and how that club currently operates. What do the fans expect? What are the players' unique needs? The same should be asked of all the other stakeholders.

It was the same for me when I stepped up to the Championship. I was operating in a different space, a space very different to the workings of League One, which now seemed quite forgiving. The pace was higher, the manager's perception of how I should be playing was different from the League One mentality and the fans' and the club's expectations were different. By truly understanding the environment I'm in I can adjust and plan accordingly. If I don't make a true assessment of the challenges ahead I'm more likely to make poor choices and start to feel demotivated if and when my game is not up to scratch.

Successful intentions

In my experience it's all too easy to have good intentions. But what we actually do often falls short of what we say we are going to do. Being able to translate healthy intentions into deeds and actions is where life is won or lost. Over the years I've learned a few tricks which help me follow through on my good intentions. Sam keeps reminding me that Woody Allen famously said: *80% of success is showing up!* Much of the work I do with Sam is about ensuring I stay on track and do the things I need to do. Naturally in every professional sport there is a lot of repetition in terms of training and recovery, and it's the same with mental practices and staying present. I constantly have to be nudged to stay on track. When I'm left to my own devices there are times when I'm more likely to lose touch with what I need to be doing.

Forming new habits requires hard work. Another hurdle to overcome when breaking old habits and forming new ones is a principle in psychology called cognitive fluency. Sam explained to me that the easier we find it to think in a certain way, the more likely we are to do so. This is because the brain often follows the easier course of action. Unfortunately for us footballers, when we lose a game we easily fall into self-criticism; the habit of beating ourselves up is very hard to get out of. In these moments mental discipline is critical. It's vital to catch the negative thoughts early, or your thinking can spiral out of control.

Accountability

Ever since I had the opportunity to play for Sporting Lisbon I've always felt I had a responsibility to work hard every day, for a couple of reasons. Growing up Setúbal made me realise how lucky I was to be given the opportunity to become a professional footballer. It was a place where furthering yourself professionally was difficult and I was presented with an opportunity to build a future in a game that I loved with my heart. Also, Ronaldo's kind act of friendship meant I was able to stay on-site in the Sporting Lisbon Academy instead of commuting all the way from home. Whenever I think of my life in football I remind myself of those who helped me to get to where I am today and those who would give anything to have the opportunity I had. I do not take for granted what I have.

At Sporting Lisbon, to ensure that I stayed on track with day-to-day training, Ronaldo and we would spur each other on. It taught me the power of a strong friendship on my overall commitment to work and train hard. I'm not sure if I would have had the same motivation if left to my own devices. Having friendly competition ensured that I kept my teeth sharp. It also made me feel accountable. I was letting Ronaldo down if I didn't do the extra training in the gym and on the football pitch with him. Of late my friend Miguel Llera became a good partner in crime to push me and make sure that I stayed hungry and motivated to train hard.

When you're trying to keep on track with good intentions, knowing there are good people backing you up is really helpful. It's much easier to exert will-power when you feel supported. Before every game I use Sam's services to make sure my mind and body are in the right place. Speaking regularly to Sam on the phone gives me an additional pressure that makes me feel accountable for working hard and doing what I'm supposed to. Regularly checking in with Ronaldo also keeps me burning in my desire to stay on track.

Although I'm quite self-contained in my mental preparation, the fans do put a healthy pressure on me to train and work hard every day. It is a privilege to be a professional footballer – the fans remind me of that all the time. For them I give my heart and soul every game. I know there are good and bad games, but I always put everything on the line for my team during those 90 minutes.

Rewards and incentives

Generally speaking, rewards and incentives are not part of my mental regime. I believe authentic long-lasting motivation has to come from inside. My inner motivation helps keep me focused on the moment-to-moment rewards and not the end game; learning to love every action and see that as the reward. There are times when I do fixate on the end result and consequently I lose my ability to experience the moment-to-moment rewards during the week.

This hit home when we got promoted to the Championship. We spent thousands of hours working hard to win promotion with nothing else on our minds. When promotion arrived, the sensation was gone within a heartbeat and we were re-grouping, getting ready for competing in the Championship Division. Although they will be wonderful memories, if my mind gets too attached to my larger achievements, I lose the richness of my day-to-day experiences. This is where the magic is and this is where the game is won or lost. Without valuing the here and now, everything suffers: motivation, confidence and the ability to maintain discipline to practise everything necessary for you to perform at your best.

After games I do however treat myself to nice food and I spend time with friends and family. Without fail during my time at Sporting Lisbon, Ronaldo and I would eat together, often pizza as a way to unwind and enjoy time to reflect on a hard day's training for a recent match.

Taking ownership

Taking ownership of my own behaviour and my own actions is something that I've learned from Ronaldo. Growing up with him and looking at every opportunity to get better as footballers has made us both leave no stone unturned in fighting to be the best we can be. From sneaking into the gym late at night, practising 1-vs-1s in almost pitch-black conditions, to studying the best running techniques, we would exhaust every avenue possible we could find to improve. Taking my performance into my own hands from a young age has put me in good stead during my professional career. I always take responsibility for my own performance and never look for blame. If I don't own my own performance I will never feel like I have the confidence to make the necessary changes to improve.

My exploration of my own psychology in football has also made me take a deeper level ownership of my performance and my behaviour. Part of my work with Sam is about being creative with all of the psychological principles we are working with. For example, taking the principle of focusing on the present moment, we would look at all areas of my life and consider the most appropriate ways to fit it into my day-to-day routines. Before I step out of the car and walk up the stadium on match day I take a series of well-controlled deep breaths to bring my mind to my body. This grounds me and makes me feel present.

Usually I will sit with Sam and come up with the ideas myself. When the principles have been conceived by me, I'm more committed to own them and build them into my regime.

Process not outcomes

To help me follow through on my healthy intentions I always try to focus on processes and not outcomes. By that I mean focusing on doing the right thing, or taking the right action in the present moment. My process table is a daily map that ensures that I rise to the challenge of the day and treat it like a performance. It keeps my mind on what I need to do so I don't become pre-occupied by what may or may not happen in the future. It comes in the form of printed sheets with questions that I score myself on every day. For example, how well did I focus on each mouthful of food when I ate (as a mindfulness goal)? How well did I keep my state of mind balanced during the day (as an engine room goal)? My process table is the blueprint and backbone of my mantra *win the day*. This process table came into its own when I was feeling a little unsettled about my place within Sheffield Wednesday. It was when I was playing under Dave Jones and struggling to get into the first team towards the end of the 2012/2013 season.

Naturally I slip up and, when my mind wanders, I can lose focus. But what is more important is that I've a mindful awareness of when I do lose discipline. It helps me get back on track, because it feels foreign and unusual when I don't go about the day in my usual, planned manner.

Keeping a tight focus on actions rather than outcomes comes from my mantra of 'winning the day'. This saying pulls me back to the here-and-now and ensures that I treat every day with the same importance as any other. Using this principle has ensured that I can find the right intensity the moment I step onto the football pitch.

State of mind check

Maintaining a check on my state of mind is critical to keeping my eye on the ball and doing what I plan. Without a balanced state of mind it is much harder to follow through and sustain discipline. For example, when I'm extremely happy, perhaps after a fantastic win, my brain naturally races into the future. In the past I've felt tempted to want to celebrate and tell everyone and discuss why and how the performance was so amazing.

But after experiencing a serious loss, my first instinct is to retreat and hide away and over-think about what went wrong.

Both emotional states take away from action, and move me into my own imagination. In order to stay on track and win the day I have to remain present and committed to the here and now.

On the subject of my emotional state of mind, I've also found that the more enjoyable and beneficial the experience is, the more likely I am to return to it naturally of my own accord. If the brain is finding something rewarding we are naturally pulled towards it.

Chunking

Breaking down goals into manageable components is part of my 'winning the day' mentality, which has helped me to feel more in control of my performances, as well as feeling more successful in my life off the pitch. Sam told me about one of the psychological theories he studied at university where Grand Chess Masters would learn to break the board down into small manageable chunks so it became easier to memorise and store their planned moves. By breaking down what I need to do each day, the weeks and months take care of themselves in terms of overall success.

Whenever I look too far ahead I can start trying too hard and eventually can become demotivated. 'Winning the day' and not letting my mind drift too far into the future is my equivalent of chunking down into small pieces and helps me achieve my goal of being the best I can be each and every moment.

Alarm clocks

One of Sam's first clients at Colchester United had a concentration problem. When the team conceded a goal his mind would fixate on what had just happened as opposed to being able to refocus on the here and now. This resulted in him getting out of position and not being alert to the current dangers in the game. To help him to stop doing this, Sam used something called environmental reminders. The technique turns common events on the football pitch into positive reminders. In his case he would use the act of the team conceding a goal as a prompt to take a deep breath and focus on his breathing. Consequently what used to be a negative trigger now becomes something constructive. You can think of them as alarm clocks going off in your head.

I use this technique regularly to ensure that I stay on track and remain mentally sharp. Here are some of the ones that I use:

1   Whenever I make a mistake I take a deep breath.
2   Every time I brush my teeth I focus on every sensation that I'm experiencing.
3   Every time I hear the whistle blow, I feel my feet on the ground and focus on the here and now.
4   Whenever I'm eating, I focus on each mouthful bringing me energy and nutrition.
5   Every time I enter my hotel room, I will create a space in which to meditate.

Being able to turn everyday occurrences on the football pitch into something positive is where the heart of the warrior mentality is for me. Making all of my experiences work for me has helped me to grow as a person and a player. The notion of 'turning straw into gold' comes to mind when I think about this strategy.

Whenever I use this technique I'm reminded that I have the capacity to turn whatever happens to me in the real world into a positive experience. My early years spent with Ronaldo taught me that everything that happens in life has value. On the face of it growing up in a bad neighbourhood and having to defend yourself against bullies and robbers has helped me to become the athlete and the man I am today. Such experiences have toughened me up and giving me the fortitude to take on the harder challenges life throws at me.

Make it easy to do

When I started working on improving my own psychology, I never imagined how difficult it would be to break old habits and form new ones. I learned that the brain loves familiarity and any move away from its norm is an up-hill battle. Whenever Sam and I work on introducing a new mental strategy into my game, we spend a significant amount of time coming up with ways to make it an instinctive part of my regime. A very simple but effective way to bridge the gap between intention and behaviour is to make sure I have easy access to the tools I need to carry out the action. This is why I build the practice of my mindful techniques into the everyday routine of my life. It means I can practise mindfulness anywhere and at any time without the requirement of a special place or special tools.

When I'm struggling to get access to things I need in order to win the day and be my best, I increase my chances of not following through on my daily positive actions. When I look back I wonder what might have happened to me if I hadn't been able to stay on site at Sporting Lisbon, and instead had to commute every day in order to train with the team. I may not have become a professional footballer. If it hadn't been for the kindness of Ronaldo, in insisting that the management team in the club made another space for me in their room, my life could have taken a completely different path. That long journey each day would have impacted on my ability to train and also made it harder to feel part of the team. These days, having easy access to the tools I need in order to train mentally, physically and spiritually has helped me to stay on track throughout my career. From the smallest things, like keeping positive mental reminders close to my bed, to having a space to pray in my house, a good gym and the immediate support of those who I love, I have what I need to make my day-to-day training fluid.

Quality not quantity

Without being disciplined during my early experiences in football I might find it hard to put the extra care and attention into the training that I do today. I often see people in the game do everything that they need to, but without the attention to detail that I think is so important. I've found that when I'm truly present and my mind, body and spirit are absorbed in what I'm doing then quality shines through.

I admit there have been times when I've felt tired and found it hard to bring 100% of my focus to the task in hand. For example if I'm in a recovery yoga session but not fully present, then I don't feel the benefits and I also stop enjoying it. This increases my chances of missing the next session too.

Without fail after training I spend some time in the gym. A good example of making sure that my focus on quality and not quantity is my work on the treadmill. When I'm on the treadmill I visualise myself running up and down the pitch, breaking down the play and getting first to the ball during typical game scenarios. It feels like the more I impress my mind with these visions the more likely they are to come true on Saturday. There have been times on the pitch when

I've experienced exactly what I'd imagined on the treadmill during training.

Quality training sessions are also important for my teammates. I remember Atdhe Nuihu looking forward to having me involved in training because I like to inject extra drive and energy into what could just be another standard training session. They can always be transformed into something more extraordinary. It's great to see his happiness and enthusiasm in all of the training sessions and I like jesting with him that I want to see him on his toes at all times!

Pep talks with the best

Staying true to myself and keeping on track has no doubt been helped by Ronaldo over the years. We will often talk at the weekends after our respective games and share our experiences. We always talk to each other as brothers and sometimes it feels like we have the same blood. The way we both conduct ourselves before and after games is very similar. Although we live in different worlds we are very much the same in our outlook and approach to life.

Feeling like we are both still side by side and sharing our journey together gives me so much strength. I've had some dark times in football and my regular pep talks with Ronaldo never fail to lift me and remind me of the winning mentality we have had ever since we were kids.

Although my best friend is in another country, regular contact with him, even if it is just a text message, gives me a boost. Even if we speak on the phone for a short period of time, it is always heart-felt. It shows that the interactions we have are about quality. We can have a deep and enriching chat that may only last five minutes.

Final thoughts

Making sure that I stick to what I'm supposed to do is where the battle is won or lost. In my experience good intentions unfortunately die hard. However, with Sam's help and reminding myself of the things I do naturally to stay disciplined I've developed a repertoire of techniques to help me to stay on track. It is not always easy and I know from experience that at times it is easy to fall off the wagon. As long as I always take ownership of my own behaviour and never look to blame anyone else I will always be in a position to get back on track.

Magic reminders

- Since working hard on my mental approach to sport I've realised how hard it is to convert good intentions into regular healthy habits.
- Talking regularly with Ronaldo puts a healthy pressure on me to work hard every day. It also reminds me of the kindness he showed me to ensure I remained in the game.
- Quality in training is more beneficial than quantity. When I put my heart and soul into my training regimes it is worth 100 times more than training done half-heartedly.
- Setting up triggers in my surrounding environment has helped me to make my positive routines a habit. It has enabled me to turn negative and ordinary experiences into positive ones.

SEVEN

MY KIND OF SUCCESS

Life is won or lost on the journey.

When you have the privilege of starting your professional career alongside the greatest football player on the planet and you've spent many years exploring your own inner psyche, you cannot help but contemplate the meaning of your journey. This chapter reflects on how I measure success and where for me the true value lies in the world of football.

Finding happiness

There have been a few special moments in my career that on reflection have seemed to flash by. During my time in League One with Sheffield Wednesday, the whole team's focus during the season was about winning promotion to the Championship Division. Fortunately with a lot of hard work and effort we managed to achieve this. When our promotion to the Championship Division was confirmed the celebrations and the partying were only fleeting moments.

It made me realise that success lies in being able to savour the journey, not just the arrival. Achievements are like the cherries on top of a beautiful cake. Although they are nice to have, they do not take away from the fact that 99% of the value for me is in the day-to-day, ie: the cake itself. After all, this is where I spend most of my time compared to the fleeting moments of celebration.

My day is won or lost, not primarily by what I achieve but how much I take from moment-to-moment experiences. When my mind was anchored on the need to win and achieve, in the past I've probably confused happiness with relief on several occasions. Unfortunately professional sport pins everything on achievement to the point that if I'm unable to perform well on the football pitch I will quickly be discarded. For me, and for other players, the happiness and success we might feel on the football pitch can get overtaken more than anything by feelings of relief. I need to secure my next contract, win the next three points and keep myself fit and healthy: these are critical to ensure I feel secure about my future in sport. I have regularly confused that feeling of utter relief with happiness.

The heavier the burden of expectation you carry through a season, the greater the sense of relief you experience at the end. Relief is a negative form of happiness as it comes after a long struggle and tough, often unpleasant experiences. Consequently, relief is usually temporary because the mind soon latches onto the next big goal and starts working towards that.

Fortunately I've learned that happiness is something completely different. I've come to appreciate that happiness is something that requires action and practice on a daily basis. Happiness certainly doesn't just come by chance – you make it by working hard. When I've worked hard and put my heart and soul into whatever I may be doing, that gives me the experience of happiness.

As you know my mantra over the last several years has been to 'win the day'. By having a working knowledge of what I need to do every day I feel like I've mentally trained to get everything I can out of each day and feel fulfilled.

It is common to fall into the trap of thinking that when I achieve a certain goal I will be happy: 'When I get to the Premiership then I will be complete', for example. My friendship with Ronaldo and my work with Sam have taught me that happiness is a choice, it is not something that we receive automatically. Ronaldo is the best player in the world, but he still wants to fight to be even better. This for me says it all: success in life is being true to yourself and living in line with your values, no matter what you are doing. The fact that he has conquered the world of football but is still as hungry as ever, shows that success and happiness cannot be about arriving at the end destination. Businessmen and women who are entrepreneurial don't stop when they make their first million, they keep going because it is in their DNA and value base to do so.

If I got to the top of the game I would be exactly the same as Ronaldo. I would still be as focused and as disciplined as ever to make sure that I keep fighting to win the day. The hunger for achievement can in some ways never be completely nourished or satisfied because there is always more to achieve. Don't get me wrong, achieving personal and professional goals is a wonderful thing. I think part of being alive and feeling successful involves reaching at least some of our goals. The danger is thinking that when I achieve my goals I will be satisfied and happy. Happiness cannot be attached to what we may or may not accomplish. Thinking like this may always feel like we are chasing something.

Being part of a team, eating, travelling, training and working together are examples of where I can find true happiness. Other times such as sneaking into the gym late at night to train, the moments of togetherness in the dressing room and working hard to pick yourself up when you are feeling down are also treasured moments.

When your mind is truly focused on the process of enjoying your time in sport and in life and when you forget about the cherries, strangely enough more seem to show up! When we won the promotion to the Championship Division and I won Player of the Year, this was mainly due to my consistency and playing every game for the club. I never let my mind think about this beforehand and just carried on enjoying my football. When I feel happy, good performances tend to follow too.

My recipe for success

For me, happiness comes from two main sources: experiencing pleasure and having meaning in your life.

Pleasure is an emotion that comes with the highs we experience day to day. There is always a lot of pleasure in being a professional footballer: the time I spend with my team-mates, being out in the fresh air, the natural chemical highs you get from exercising, being admired by the fans, the buzz of playing in front of thousands of people, travelling to different parts of the country and the highs of celebrating important victories. But if it becomes only about pleasure, it is easy to constantly want to seek it. Pleasure is something great to experience but if my life was only pleasure-seeking I know I would never quite feel nourished. This is where meaning plays an important part.

Having meaning in my life comes from my values. I've spoken about the warrior mentality and what it means to meet challenges with the right mindset; there is some detail about this near the end of Chapter 5. Most of my meaning and happiness comes from my family and close friends, as well as the close connection with my religious faith. Having a sense of these values and the important areas in my life makes everything I do richer and gives it purpose. My experiences have a greater level of significance and hold deeper value than they would if they were enjoyed just at an emotional level.

If my *only* aim in playing Championship football was to make more money and receive greater respect as a footballer, my ambition would lack meaning. However, if my goal was to challenge myself, push outside my comfort zone, look to support my family with the money I earn and enjoy a change in style of football, then my ambitions have meaning – and also, they can be sustained. If I achieve the first goals, I may get a quick hit of pleasure but it will soon be gone. This is not to say that getting paid more and being respected a little more as an accomplished footballer isn't nice; they are pleasurable of course, but don't have real meaning. However, when goals hold deeper meaning and I accomplish them they mean so much more when I achieve them.

Unfortunately football provides rewards not for how you were on the journey but where you arrived. It rewards outcomes and results, not processes. Despite this I think Ronaldo and I are two footballers who are deeply connected with meaning and our values. Even though Ronaldo is such a great footballer I know that he would still have the same values and work ethic at whatever level he was playing. There is no doubt about it: when meaning and value is found in what you do, everything feels richer and more rewarding.

Pleasurable experiences are far more intense and lasting when you have meaning in your life. Getting promoted to the Championship, receiving Player of the Year awards, and seeing all the Wednesday fans celebrating Semedo Day (as I explain later) all felt richer because I have firm values and strong inner foundations. The meaning and value I've gained from some of my experiences in football are up there with the enjoyment players get when they win the World Cup.

Happiness and success

I've seen over the years how closely linked happiness is to success. The happier I am, the more productive I am in my work and the more successful I am in life generally. I've also observed that the more successful I am the happier I am, and so the two feed one another. When I make my inner well-being my priority, the football often takes care of itself. My investment in learning about human psychology and sport psychology has given me a fresh perspective on what it truly means to be happy. While learning about what I need for myself I've found I play better football as a by-product. A large part of feeling successful is being able to look in the mirror and know that I'm giving 100% in everything that I do. As long as I know this, any positive outcomes from my labours feel like a bonus.

Gratitude

Whenever I'm in the mindset of always chasing my goals and my dreams, I stop appreciating what I actually have in the here and now. Because my mind is always on the next big achievement, I lose sight of all of the great things that are going on in the present moment. This is even more noticeable when I'm not playing well. It strikes me that so much of my day-to-day happiness can get tied up in my performances. When they're not going my way, it is easy to want to retreat and shut down, hoping that the next match will replace the negative feeling with a positive one.

I remind myself what a privilege it is to play football professionally and how millions of people would give their right arm to have such an opportunity. One strategy Sam and I worked on was to write a list of five things that I felt grateful for. Some of the items I came up with were: being a professional footballer, my family, having somewhere nice to live, my health and my friends. On other occasions I would write down simple things like having a nice car, living in a great city and being able to travel home to Portugal regularly. It doesn't really matter too much what you write down, as long as it encourages you to move away from thinking negatively. As Sam and I have discussed, we definitely draw to ourselves more of what we focus on. If the mind is pre-occupied with all of the things that you don't want it draws more of these negative experiences into your life. This gratitude exercise has definitely helped me to not let negative thinking take over after a poor performance.

There is nothing worse than losing the rest of your weekend because your mind is still dwelling on Saturday's let-down. By making a conscious effort to move my mind onto the positives, it becomes easier to have an enjoyable weekend rather than one where I'm ruminating and worrying about my last performance.

It's amazing how small actions like making a gratitude list can change my train of thought and have an impact on how my day goes. In some ways the gratitude exercise snaps me out of my negative thinking. It's a bit like splashing my face with cold water: it's a much needed wake-up call. Before and after matches, and before I go to sleep are the most common times that I reflect on what I have and practise gratitude. Again it's so easy to get caught up in always wanting more. Strangely enough, it's my experience that when I take a step back and value and recognise what I currently have, I end up attracting more rewarding experiences.

I think it comes with the territory when you're fiercely competitive and always wanting to push the limits and strive for the best. This over-desire has got in the way of my progress at times which is why reflecting on what I'm grateful for and what I've achieved allows me to find balance.

Stepping off the roller-coaster

Life in football is a roller-coaster. I've had to find a way to manage the ups and downs in order to stay competitive in the game. We all experience great victories and great failures in life. The art for me is being able to detach from them, and move on quickly. When I think of my most consistent strings of performances in my career they have come from being able to come down and re-group quickly after a performance, whether it was a win, lose or draw.

Not only this, but how I manage my inner enemies is the difference between succeeding and failing. Irrespective of all of the blessings I have in my life I will admit there are times when my happiness has been governed by how my football was going. I'm sure that for all professional footballers day-to-day well-being is directly related to how they are performing in training and on the pitch. It is easier said than done to avoid this, especially when the gains are so high if you're consistently performing well. However, I whole-heartedly believe that I've released some of the pressure from the world of football by developing other interests outside of sport. Family is the most important thing in my life. Coming home to those you love helps you to detach from the last performance and ground yourself in the wider world. Spending time with my children and my wife has given me the inner strength that we all need. Naturally if my career was the only thing in my life, I would start placing more pressure on myself to make it work. Winning football matches as my only source of meaning in the world would leave me feeling very vulnerable and isolated when results don't go my way.

The modern day religion

Football provides the perfect platform to inspire everyone in and around the game. As a professional footballer you realise the power that football holds in communities and society as a whole. In some ways football has become like a modern day religion. Fans turn up every week to get behind their team and support them for a whole afternoon. You see them put their heart and soul on the line for their team. At times the fans' support is breathtaking.

If I wasn't a footballer, the next best job for me would be a musician. I think this is because music has the power to bring happiness to the world just like football does. I believe music helps people go through difficult times and changes people in positive ways. There are times when I'm feeling down that music gives me a much needed lift.

As a performer when I step out into stadiums across the country I know it's a privilege to entertain thousands of fans. What an honour, to get to paid to do something you love. Throughout my journey in football, I've learned more about the importance about being a good role-model, because the fans idolise their footballers.

At all of the clubs I've played for the incredible support I've had from the fans has been a blessing. The passion that the UK fans have for the game is unbelievable at times. I was made fully aware of this when I signed for Charlton Athletic; the fans blew me away and made me feel so welcome for every minute I played for the club. They even made a song for me, which made me feel part of the Charlton family. Usually it's the creative and offensive players who get songs made for them. So for me to get this treatment was very special and it made me feel very proud. So every time I stepped out onto the football pitch I would give everything for the fans. The love they gave me at Charlton is something I will never forget and will always carry with me.

Playing for Sheffield Wednesday is the pinnacle of my career; this is my home. The club also has the best dressing-room of any club I've ever played in! I remember once when I was playing against Sheffield Wednesday in League One, I saw what the fans were like and knew that I had to play for them one day. Looking over at the opposition fans I felt an immediate special connection and knew that it was the club for me. Six months later I was there, and I believe God brought me to this amazing club. It's unbelievable, because I loved Charlton too and I never thought it was physically possible to love a club even more. I had no real reason to leave Charlton, I was in the process of renewing my contract, but something inside me knew that playing for Sheffield Wednesday was my destiny. It is like God brought me to my true love, like finding your soul-mate. This is how I feel about Sheffield Wednesday.

Doing my best with the tools I've been given is my main priority in life and in sport. I think it is a general principle we can all have, whatever we do in our lives. If I can transmit that to the fans, in some ways that is more important to me than winning and losing. Being the best version of ourselves possible I believe will be the benchmark of whether we have won in life or not.

I think this country can be proud of saying that they have the best football league in the world. I think the fans make football in this country the best in the world. Their passion for the game is unbelievable. This country may not have the best national team in the world, but I believe the UK is the home of football.

Through football you can change the world. How many fans turn up to stadiums every week across the world and how many fans tune into Sky Sports every week? Football is special because of the global audience it commands. The sport provides an unbelievable vehicle to send positive messages across the world and inspire younger generations.

Bradford's brilliance

One of the greatest examples of football clubs having power over communities is Bradford City's rejuvenation under my old boss Phil Parkinson. Bradford as a city has been struggling to recover after a deep recession. With high unemployment in the area, for many of the local people it was watching their Bradford City play on a Saturday that gave them a means to escape from a lot of the difficulties that surrounded them.

Seeing Bradford City win promotion to League One, get to a League Cup final and very recently beat the Premiership Champions at Stamford Bridge lifted the whole city from what I hear. It was another reminder of the power football has in this country. Even with minimal financial resources, having a strong set of values, and a good work ethic within the team, the impossible can be achieved. The right mentality is the key, you cannot put a price on true heart and guts. I know that I will never have the natural talent of Ronaldo but with the right mentality alone amazing things can be achieved. Bradford City is an example of this in the Cup run and the recent victory over Chelsea.

Semedo Day

It was on 17 November 2012 against Nottingham Forest that the Sheffield Wednesday fans organised Semedo Day for me. To date it is my most profound and heart-warming experience in football. I'm truly blessed to have experienced something so magical. I remember stepping onto the football pitch in Nottingham and seeing thousands of fans with my face! They were wearing masks made from a photo of me. The fans were also waving Portuguese flags to add to this incredible tribute. What a sight! All I could hear were the fans chanting my song, 'He's Magic you know' throughout the afternoon; it nearly brought a tear to my face.

Although we lost that game it will always be one of the most memorable and special days in football for me. I never expected anything like this to happen in my career, which made it all the more amazing. From the bottom of my heart I want to thank all of the fans for organising such an incredible tribute. If I'm being completely honest, words fail me. Semedo Day still hasn't quite sunk in and I don't think it ever will. The way everybody has treated me at Sheffield Wednesday is unbelievable, not just on special days like the Semedo Day, but every day.

The measure of friendship

Ronaldo has set the benchmark for what it means to be a true friend. Whenever I talk with Ronaldo I feel a different kind of friendship. He is like a brother and part of my family. He inspires me to be great and is a massive part of my life. His fight to keep me in the Sporting Lisbon residence changed my life forever and for that I will be grateful until I die. The help I've had from friends and managers at key moments will sit with me in my heart forever. When I see some of my friends end up in jail or die it makes me realise how my life could have taken a completely different path if it wasn't for Ronaldo.

There are so many special memories of when Ronaldo and I have laughed so hard. It's moments like that when I feel true happiness. At Sporting Lisbon in the mornings I was the only one to wake up at 7 a.m. and go to school. The others in the room including Ronaldo would aim to go to school for 10 a.m. I would get up quietly, and take my clothes from the wardrobe and try not to disturb anyone. On one occasion Ronaldo saw me getting ready and stood up out of bed and asked me where I was going. I said 'I am going to school' and his response was 'why are you going to school? We are going to be the best footballers in the world!' I reminded him that if we don't go to school our boss at Sporting Lisbon would not be happy and punish us. Ronaldo insisted I stayed with him, encouraging me to get more sleep. To this day we joke that if I had gone to school I would have been a world genius in my field. Perhaps a leading doctor, or an award-winning writer? So we both know that Ronaldo is the reason I didn't become that top scientist who solved the world's problems!

There is still so much to learn about myself, my profession and life as a whole. I want to keep being curious and driven by the desire to be better. This will never change. What Ronaldo and I learned growing up is an understanding of what we can control and what we can't control. We put all of our efforts into what we could actually do, such as sneaking into the gym late at night to train, and studying the local runners in order to improve our speed. Nothing was ever taken for granted; each day was a gift and an opportunity for us to hone our trade as professional footballers.

A symbol of unity

A really special moment that sticks with me as a symbol of my true friendship with Ronaldo was when he presented me with his first Chanel designer watch he bought for himself. Ronaldo bought this watch when he knew that for the rest of his life he would be a professional footballer. It was just before he signed for Manchester United.

Receiving Ronaldo's first watch that he bought for himself blew me away, I was deeply touched. Usually I don't use the watch because it is so special to me, but when I go to see him I wear it. I keep that watch safe at all times. In some ways it felt like he dedicated something to me as a friend. It is very heart-warming when I think about it. He knows that I will always cherish this watch and take good care of it for ever.

Mentors and friends

I have drawn inspiration from a wide range of people I've encountered in life, and have found that I don't have to rely on one person for advice and guidance. Having a community of trusted individuals in my life is important. Everyone has an opinion, and being able to build up a broader view on a situation is always helpful. Besides Phil Parkinson and Sam Kotadia, who I've spoken about already, there are many people who have come into my life and helped me in so many ways to find myself. There are many who have challenged me and encouraged me to look at the world in new ways. Other than Ronaldo there are several influential people in my life I would not hesitate to call on for advice.

A warm welcome

When I first moved to the UK and signed for Charlton Athletic Football Club I met Nicky Weaver and Paddy McCarthy, who both signed for the club at the same time as me. During this period the three of us stayed at the same hotel for almost a month and spent a lot of time together both on and off the pitch. They were positive influences in my life as even though my English language skills were very poor they always encouraged me to join them in their daily activities, and never let me feel alone. Every single day for example they would take me to training sessions, encourage me to chill with them at the hotel pool and invite me to dinner. They would buy me DVDs too and no matter where they were going, even if it was just popping to the shops, they would knock at my hotel bedroom door and take me with them whether I needed to go or not. They were so very kind and great company too. I'll always remember our first training session together. It started at 10 a.m. and finished at lunch-time. In Portugal my daily schedule involved morning and late afternoon training sessions, enabling me to go out for lunch and eat well at mid-day before resting in the afternoon because the hot climate stopped us from playing. In England, however, totally unknown to myself at first, the training schedule was quite different with daily training sessions in the morning and early afternoon whatever the weather. So when my first morning training session with Charlton Athletic finished I took myself off for a large lunch (I eat a lot, especially after working out), so I couldn't quite believe my eyes when afterwards they suddenly came to take me back to training again so quickly. I couldn't explain to them in English that I was too full to start training again straight away, so I just pointed at my stomach. It was so funny. They took me to a really hard running session and just helped me get through it. I felt pretty awful afterwards and very quickly learnt to change my eating habits. Together we enjoyed some great moments during these times, which I will never forget and for which I'm truly thankful. After some time my life as a footballer in England suddenly changed, which is common in our industry, as Paddy left Charlton Athletic for Crystal Palace and Nicky left for Sheffield Wednesday.

Following Nicky's departure we stayed in touch and texted each other all the time, but the next time Charlton played Sheffield Wednesday he was injured and didn't play. I felt the passion at Hillsborough so strongly that day, it was as if something was calling me to play there. So when the first real opportunity came for me to move to Sheffield Wednesday I called Nicky straight after my meeting with the manager and asked him all about life at the club. He told me that I would love Sheffield Wednesday more than any other club I've ever loved in my whole life. He spoke very positively and passionately about it, and when he talked about the fans it was obvious he felt he played for the best club in the country.

Nicky Weaver is an influential figure in my life. It was when I became a dad that I built an even stronger relationship with him. Nicky is now working as a coach in the youth team at Sheffield Wednesday and every time he sees me I'm greeted with happiness. The love and care I feel from him is warming and at times I feel like his younger brother. It's another example of how Sheffield Wednesday is like my family.

I'd always dreamt of coming to the UK and playing English football. It was Alan Pardew, the manager of Charlton Athletic, who gave me my first shot at English football. I believe if you ask most Portuguese footballers they would say they want to play in English football: 90% of the football players in my home country will say this for sure. There is also great respect for the Championship Division in English football in Portugal, despite it being a tier below the top league.

I remember Alan Pardew being a guy who was big on motivation. When we were going through a tough period he got the whole team together to watch a motivational video on one occasion in preparation to the game. I cannot remember the exact game but I can recall the team gathering and watching the big screen in the dressing room and seeing a preview of our match with the backdrop of the Champions League theme music. It is always a big night for any footballer to play in the Champions League and his strategy made us feel we were gearing up for such a match. We ended up winning the game! I think this is one of Pardew's main strengths: he knows how to fire up his team. When he got the job at Newcastle they were struggling, but he was able to guide them nearly to Champions League football. I have no doubt that a lot of this was down to his man-motivational skills. He is also very mentally tough and knows how to deal with difficult environments exceptionally well. This is certainly what I've observed from him as a player.

When I arrived at Charlton I couldn't speak any English. Fortunately for me I met someone who worked for the Charlton's Community: a guy called Walter Antonis. He was from Portugal and immediately I started talking with him regularly. On one occasion Alan Pardew saw me talking to Walter and wondered what language we were using. We were speaking for a lengthy period of time and he became even more curious. To Pardew's credit he could see the value of me being able to communicate with one of our colleagues and he promoted Walter from his post as a community coach to a member of his first team coaching staff. Consequently Walter made it possible for me to learn English much faster. He was by my side most of the time in my first season at Charlton.

Walter was a professional footballer too. By coincidence I watched him play in my home town Setúbal, but when I met him for the first time in the UK I didn't realise he was that player. It was like we were meant to meet. He continues to give me advice today and because of the pivotal role he played in helping me to adjust to my new life in the UK I asked him to be godfather to my two sons Denzel and Jason.

I have been very blessed with my clubs' football managers, and learned something from all of them. As well as experiencing the man-management brilliance of Phil Parkinson and Alan Pardew, I've also been helped by several other managers.

Chris Powell, formerly of Charlton Athletic, is a very good manager. His approach to the game is so fresh his enthusiasm is infectious. At Charlton he wanted to train with us as if he was still a player. During our training with Chris we would regularly organise 5-vs-5 matches in which he would get involved. He did an amazing job at Charlton; I don't think he deserved to be sacked. He got them back to the Championship which was a difficult task to do. That shows how good he is, too.

Of all the managers I've played under, Gary Megson is the one I learned the most from. Having Megson in the dressing room is like being with a lion. His mentality of winning at any cost is unbelievable. We had a tremendous time with him at Sheffield Wednesday. He was the man who showed great belief in my abilities, and I recall he travelled to London personally to meet with me just before I moved from Charlton to Sheffield Wednesday to say he wanted me in his team. That meant a lot to me.

Thanks to God I've always had good relationships with my managers. Megson for sure is someone you don't forget and people who have worked with him carry his influence always. Even now I hear his voice encouraging me to fight until I die!

In some ways Megson and Ronaldo are similar. For both of them losing is simply unacceptable. Nobody wants to lose, but these two just don't admit the possibility of losing. Losing is not in their vocabulary.

My former boss at Sheffield Wednesday Dave Jones was completely different from Megson. Jones was at peace and very calm, whilst Megson wore his heart on his sleeve. Dave Jones had an excellent assistant manager in Terry Burton, who helped Jones a great deal, and they complemented each other. Dave Jones knows about football for sure: he has been around the game for a long time and you can feel his experience when you work with him. If you are doing well, you have a good life under Dave Jones. He was the manager I've had most success with. Thanks to him we won promotion to the Championship Division, which was new to me.

My current manager Stuart Gray is a fantastic guy. Since he came in as an assistant manager I've seen what an incredible person he is. When Dave Jones left Sheffield Wednesday and Gray took over I learned he was a manager who goes the extra mile to treat everyone in the club exactly the same, irrespective of whether or not you are on form. Whether it's the Under-18s or senior players like Chris Kirkland, he is the same with everyone. It is the first time in my professional career that I've been in a dressing room where no one has a bad word to say about the head coach. It is so easy for the players who are not being picked to criticise the manager. With head coach Stuart Gray this does not happen: he always has his reasons and explains exactly why he has made his decision in such way that you don't go away feeling too despondent if you are not picked. Obviously you are disappointed, but the way he explains himself makes it easier to take. He is the most complete manager I've worked with.

A good coach like Gray doesn't take you away from the day-to-day action when you are not in the starting eleven, and ensures that you don't feel lonely. Gray pulls the whole team together and everyone finds it a pleasure to work with him. He is at the training ground every day and always gets involved in what we are doing. This makes you feel good and

ensures that every day you are playing with the right intensity. His sessions are great: they make everybody feel alive.
After all, he has been around many top managers and has
learned from them all, bringing this experience to his mana-
gerial style.

Leonel Pontes grew up in Madeira, like Ronaldo. He was
my first manager at Sporting Lisbon and has known me
since I was seven years old; I grew up with his guiding hand
throughout my whole youth development. Every day, Leonel
would give himself mind, body and spirit to all of his players.
He had a huge influence on both me and Ronaldo in the early
years. He always gave us good advice and often after training
we would go for dinner together. We still speak together
regularly and his advice for me is never to change who I am,
never compromise my work ethic and always fight hard to
compete every day.

Leonel is an unbelievable guy, one of the greatest professionals I've had the pleasure of working with. His discipline
and work ethic shone like a guiding light for me. Leonel was
assistant manager alongside Paulo Bento, and is now the
assistant manager for Portugal. On one occasion he called me
straight after playing Rochdale in the F.A. Cup. It was a rare
televised game that he was able to watch in Spain and said to
me how proud he was to see me playing so well. He said to me
that 'you are an example in my life to follow', and to hear that
means the world to me, it makes me feel so proud. To hear
this from a big man like him is incredible.

Because I was out of contract in the summer at Sheffield
Wednesday he was very keen to sign me for Marítimo, the
club he had just started managing. Although this offer was
very flattering at the time, again I knew my home was at
Sheffield Wednesday. As I've said before, it's like when you
find the woman you want to marry and you know she is the

one for you: this is how I feel about Sheffield Wednesday. The club is my soul-mate in the football world.

However, I do hope the future brings Leonel and me together, either in the coaching department or while I'm still playing. Surely he will be a top manager and we all wish the very best for this guy.

One of my deepest and most recent friendships in the game is with the Spanish centre back Miguel Llera. He is one of the greatest professionals I've worked with. He came to Charlton six years ago, and spoke Spanish which is very close to my first language Portuguese, giving us that common ground to communicate and helping us develop a close friendship. We are both family men and both know where the true value of life lies. Being around Miguel has also sharpened my mentality of winning the day. In ways similar to how Ronaldo and I would support each other, Miguel and I push each other to work hard every day. Certainly I learned a new level of professionalism by working with Miguel, who is coming up to 36 years of age and still playing professional football at a high level. This is an achievement in itself. I think this is because of his desire to look after himself in every way possible and always improve. Although we are now both playing at different clubs we still make sure we go to watch each other play when we have the opportunity. Our kids are growing up together which pulls our families even closer. Just as Ronaldo is a friend for life, Miguel is another.

There are so many strong characters in the current Sheffield Wednesday dressing room. One key figure who stands out and has had a profound effect on my game is Chris Kirkland. He has played football to the highest level and has a real passion and hunger to share his knowledge and experience with everyone. He wants to help everybody and lift all of his team-mates both on and off the football pitch. Seeing the way he works has inspired me always to stay on track and win every day. He is a player who will never give up. Every day he fights for his place. On one occasion I remember Chris telling me that he believed in me and that he saw me as a great role-model. Hearing this makes you feel like you can run through brick walls. I hope I'm always able to draw on Chris's wisdom and experience for as long as I'm playing professional football.

The world of football has given me a great opportunity to meet some incredible people who I hope will be actively involved in my life for many years to come.

Breaking the mould

Ronaldo and I expect to play for at least another six years. It was only a few weeks Ronaldo was telling me that he feels like a 25-year-old again! We both have a desire to change the idea that when you pass the age of 30 your career is winding down. In January 2015 we met in Madrid and we were talking about how we want to finish football on our own terms and not because the game wants to retire us when we hit 35 or 36. When you see Ryan Giggs making the age of 40 as a professional footballer, you realise there is no reason why Ronaldo and I cannot do the same thing. Having a common goal with the world's greatest player gives me extra strength and as brothers it pulls us both closer together.

The future

I still have many professional playing years ahead of me. As long as I continue to apply everything I've talked about in the book I'm hoping there is plenty more that I can get out of the game. Working with Sam and developing my game alongside Ronaldo has made me develop a keener interest in the coaching side of the game. When I'm out on the football pitch and in the dressing room, I'm always looking to support my team-mates. I try to do everything I can to bring the best out of them.

Most of this is a psychological game. In the simplest sense, if those around you feel good they will naturally play better football and make life a little easier for you on the pitch. I get such a buzz when something I say or do raises the game of those around me. In the future I do see myself becoming a football manager because I've experienced at first-hand how much pleasure I get from inspiring teams and individuals.

Final thoughts

This book is a gift to all of those who love the way I am and the way I live. I want to share my way of life and show everyone that we all have a lot in common. I don't feel like I'm anything special or anything different. I believe whatever we do for a living we are all the same.

Working hard with Ronaldo from a young age has encouraged me to turn negative experiences into positive ones, be mindful and accepting of inevitable pain from to time, push outside the comfort zone, and show compassion and support to my fellow competitors.

There have been so many magic moments in my career and no doubt I will continue to experience more of them. The Semedo Day that the Sheffield Wednesday fans organised, beating Sheffield United in the local derby to help us secure promotion to the Championship Division, and my endless adventures and experiences with Ronaldo hold some of the magic I've experienced in football to date.

Even at the age of 30 I'm still learning and still getting better. As long I'm able to have this mindset I will keep growing and living life to the full.

Magic reminders

- Being grateful for every moment I have in football has amplified my day-to-day satisfaction of being involved in the game.
- As long as I'm being true to myself I will feel happy and I will continue to be successful.
- The world of football has exposed me to so many wonderful and inspiring people. Many of them will be friends and colleagues for life.
- The Semedo Day organised by the fans of Sheffield Wednesday was one of the most beautiful experiences I've ever had. It's a reminder of the power football has in modern society and the responsibility I have as a player to be a good role-model.
- Alongside my friend Ronaldo I plan on playing up until the age of 40.
- Sheffield Wednesday is my home!

My Sheffield Wednesday family

Thank you, all of the team-mates I've had along the way, especially my team-mates at Sheffield Wednesday. Everyone involved in my footballing journey will always be very special to me. Thank you, all the coaches from the academy all the way through to the first team. Thank you, to all of my managers, the kit-men, the ladies at the club who look after the launderette, the club chef, the groundsmen, and the security team at the club. I especially want to thank the fans at this wonderful club, the Chairman, the Vice Chairman, the directors and the Club Secretary who have built such a wonderful family at Sheffield Wednesday.

NOTES

NOTES

NOTES

NOTES

NOTES

NOTES